6/20/17
$29.95

EXPERIMENTS FOR FUTURE
FORENSIC
SCIENTISTS

ROBERT GARDNER
AND JOSHUA CONKLIN

Enslow Publishing
101 W. 23rd Street

Published in 2017 by Enslow Publishing, LLC.
101 W. 23rd Street, Suite 240, New York, NY 10011

Library of Congress Cataloging-in-Publication Data

Names: Gardner, Robert.
Title: Experiments for future forensic scientists / Robert Gardner and Joshua Conklin.
Description: New York : Enslow Publishing, 2017. | Series: Experiments for future STEM professionals | Includes bibliographical references and index.
Identifiers: ISBN 9780766082021 (library bound)
Subjects: LCSH: Forensic sciences—Juvenile literature. | Forensic sciences—Experiments—Juvenile literature.
Classification: LCC HV8073.8 G368 2017 | DDC 363.25—dc23

Printed in the United States of America

To Our Readers: We have done our best to make sure all website addresses in this book were active and appropriate when we went to press. However, the author and the publisher have no control over and assume no liability for the material available on those websites or on any websites they may link to. Any comments or suggestions can be sent by e-mail to customerservice@enslow.com.

Photo Credits: Cover, Robert Kneschke/Shutterstock.com (forensic scientist), Timof/ Shutterstock.com (lab), Titov Nikolai/Shutterstock.com (atom symbol), elic/Shutterstock .com (magenta geometric background throughout book), Zffoto/Shutterstock.com (white textured background throughout book), pp. 54, 61 Hein Nouwens/Shutterstock.com (pelvis), Sebastian Kaulitzki/Shutterstock.com (femur), p. 56 stihii/Shutterstock.com.

Illustrations by Joseph Hill.

CONTENTS

INTRODUCTION

Forensic science involves using science for purposes related to law. It draws upon many scientific disciplines—psychology, pathology, toxicology, physical anthropology, physics, chemistry, biology, and geology, to name a few. Consequently, scientists from many different fields can be involved with forensic science and can contribute to solving crimes. Often forensic science plays a part in a court trial where the evidence requires an understanding of science. It also involves investigating and analyzing crime scenes and the evidence collected there.

WHAT DO FORENSIC SCIENTISTS DO?

A forensic scientist seeks to provide a fair and unbiased use of information to determine essential facts and the truth as they relate to crimes. He or she uses science to assist lawyers, judges, and juries in understanding the science related to the evidence surrounding a crime.

Forensic scientists must be able to make detailed notes and write clear and accurate reports about specific evidence. They must be capable of making decisions about which facts or pieces of evidence are relevant. In some cases, the forensic scientist may find it necessary to visit the crime scene to gather evidence or confirm or deny police reports.

As a forensic scientist, you would use your knowledge of science to help solve crimes. You would probably be employed by a police department and would spend much of your time analyzing clues and evidence found at crime scenes. You would also spend time testifying in court and explaining to judges and jurors the science involved as it relates to the crime.

The following are some brief descriptions of the different roles of a forensic scientist. You might decide to specialize in one of these areas.

Accountant: Interprets and analyzes financial information related to crimes.

Chemist: Carries out analysis of such things as blood, firearm and bomb residues, and drugs found at crime scenes.

Dactyloscopist: Collects, analyzes, and identifies fingerprints.

Engineer: Identifies the causes of accidents or catastrophes.

Entomologist: Estimates time of death using evidence such as body temperature, insects, insect eggs, or larvae on the corpse.

Geologist: Analyzes soil, minerals, plants, and debris at a crime scene.

Odontologist: Identifies a body by comparing the victim's teeth to dental record; analyzes bite marks to help identify a criminal.

Physical anthropologist: Investigates human and other skeletal remains to determine or estimate gender, age, and time of death.

Technician: Analyses evidence collected at crime scenes.

TO BECOME A FORENSIC SCIENTIST

The path to becoming a forensic scientist should begin in high school. Your courses should include biology, physics, chemistry, earth science, computer science, and all the mathematics courses offered. It should also include English and other courses that require writing because as a forensic scientist, you will have to write clear and concise crime-scene and evidence reports.

Forensic scientists are creative, analytical, inquisitive, and attentive to details. They enjoy solving problems and thinking creatively. They must also be able to communicate their thoughts and ideas clearly, both orally and in writing. If you have these abilities, then a career in forensic science might be for you.

There are many kinds of forensic scientists. You will have time to consider the area you wish to focus on while studying the basic courses in a forensic science curriculum. During your senior year in high school, you should talk with a guidance counselor about colleges that offer a curriculum leading to a career in forensic science. You will probably major in criminology in college. Many college and university criminology departments offer courses in forensic science … Then, to be better prepared as a forensic scientist, you may want to spend two years in a graduate program leading to a master's degree in forensic science (MSFS).

SOME SUGGESTIONS BEFORE YOU BEGIN EXPERIMENTING

At times, as you do the experiments, demonstrations, and other activities in this book, you may need the help of a partner. It would be best to work with someone who also enjoys experimenting. In that way, you will both enjoy the process. **If any safety issues or danger are involved in doing an experiment, you will be warned. In some cases, to avoid danger, you will be asked to work with an adult. Please do so**. We don't want you to take any chances that could lead to injury.

Like any good scientist, you will find it helpful to record your ideas, notes, data, and conclusions in a notebook. By doing so, you can keep track of the information you gather and the conclusions you reach. Taking notes will allow you to refer to things you have done and help in future projects. It may also prove useful as a reference during college admission interviews.

THE SCIENTIFIC METHOD

Many forensic scientists are involved in researching crimes and crime scenes as they seek clues that can lead to solving a crime. They ask questions, make careful observations, and conduct research. Different crimes require different approaches. Depending on the crime, one approach is likely to be better than another. Using evidence surrounding a murder requires different techniques than those used to investigate the forging of a document, but each demands an understanding of how science is done.

Despite the differences, all scientists use a similar, general approach to research called the scientific method. In most research where science is involved, some or all of the following steps are used: making an observation, formulating a question, making a hypothesis (one possible answer to the question) and a prediction (an if-then statement), designing and conducting one or more experiments, analyzing the results in order to reach conclusions about your hypothesis, and accepting or rejecting the hypothesis.

As a young forensic scientist, you might wonder how to start an experiment. When you observe something at a crime scene, you may become curious and ask a question. Your question, which could arise from observing some aspect of a crime scene or a piece of evidence, may be answered by a well-designed investigation. Once you have a question, you can make a hypothesis. Your hypothesis is a possible answer to the question (what you think will happen). Once you have a hypothesis, it is time to design an experiment to test a consequence of your hypothesis.

In most cases, it is appropriate to do a controlled experiment. This means having two groups that are treated exactly the same except for the single factor being tested. That factor is called a variable. For example, suppose your question is, "Was this fingerprint, which was found at the scene of a crime, left by the suspect? "Your hypothesis is that the fingerprint will match that of the suspect, so you compare the fingerprint from the crime scene with the fingerprints of the suspect. If they match, your hypothesis is proven to be correct. If, instead, the fingerprint matches that of the victim, your hypothesis was incorrect.

Two other terms are often used in science—*dependent* and *independent variables*. The dependent variable depends on the value of the independent variable. For example, the area of a plot of land depends on the length and width of the plot. Here, the dependent value is the area. It depends on the length and width, the independent variables.

SAFETY FIRST

Safety is important in science and engineering. Certain rules apply when doing experiments. Some of the rules below may seem obvious to you, others may not, but it is important that you follow all of them.

1. Have an adult help you whenever this book, or any other, so advises.
2. Wear eye protection and closed-toe shoes (not sandals). Tie back long hair.
3. Do not eat or drink while experimenting. Never taste substances being used (unless instructed to do so).

4. Do not touch chemicals with your bare hands. Use tools, such as spatulas, to transfer chemicals from place to place.

5. The liquid in some thermometers is mercury (a dense liquid metal). It is dangerous to touch mercury or breathe mercury vapor. Mercury thermometers have been banned in many states. When doing experiments that require you to measure temperature, use only electronic or non-mercury thermometers, such as those filled with alcohol. If you have a mercury thermometer in the house, **ask an adult** if it can be taken to a local thermometer exchange location.

6. Conduct only those experiments that are described in this book or those that have been approved by **an adult**.

7. Maintain a serious attitude while conducting experiments. Don't be careless or joke around.

8. Before beginning an experiment, read all the instructions carefully and be sure you understand them.

9. Remove all items not needed for the experiment from your work space.

10. At the end of every activity, clean all materials used and put them away. Then wash your hands thoroughly with soap and water.

CRIME DETECTION KIT

You may find it useful to put together a crime detection kit before you start experimenting. You will find the materials useful as you do the experiments in this book. Your kit can contain the following materials: magnifying glass, Super Glue, forceps, microscope and slides (optional), ninhydrin or graphite powder, graduated cylinder or metric measuring cup, cotton, and wide, clear plastic tape.

The chapters that follow contain experiments and information that every future forensic scientist should know. They will also help you to decide if working as a forensic scientist is a career you might like to pursue.

CHAPTER ONE

DACTYLOSCOPY: STUDYING FINGERPRINTS

The basic principle on which forensic science is founded is that a criminal always takes something to the scene of a crime and that something is always left. Or in the words of Edmund Locard, the father of forensic science, "Every contact leaves a trace."

As early as the 1850s, William Herschel, a British magistrate stationed in India (which was a British colony at the time), realized that fingerprints are unique. He used fingerprints to identify illiterate natives who signed their names using a fingerprint, and prevent fraud. The natives would often try to collect their pay twice. After Herschel began using fingerprints as a means of identification, the fraud ceased.

During the early twentieth century, police began to use fingerprints to identify criminals.

In 1924, fingerprint records from Fort Leavenworth Prison and the Bureau of Investigation were merged when the Federal Bureau of Investigation (FBI) was established. Today the FBI has hundreds of millions of fingerprints on file.

Fingerprints were first used to convict a criminal in the United States in 1910. Thomas Jennings was accused of killing Clarence Hiller while robbing Hiller's home. At trial it was revealed that shortly before the robbery, Hiller had painted his porch railing. Jennings had touched the railing with his left hand. The fingerprints found in the paint matched Jennings' fingerprints. After seeing the fingerprint evidence, the jury found Jennings guilty.

Fingerprints are always sought by police when investigating a crime scene. The reason is that no two people, not even identical twins, have the same fingerprints. Fingerprints are truly unique and provide indisputable forensic evidence.

In this chapter you will begin to learn how forensic scientists use fingerprints to solve crimes.

EXPERIMENT

YOUR FINGERPRINTS

In this experiment you will take a close look at your own fingerprints.

1. Turn your hand palm side up. Look at the ends of your fingers

THINGS YOU WILL NEED

- **magnifying glass (convex lens)**
- **other people**

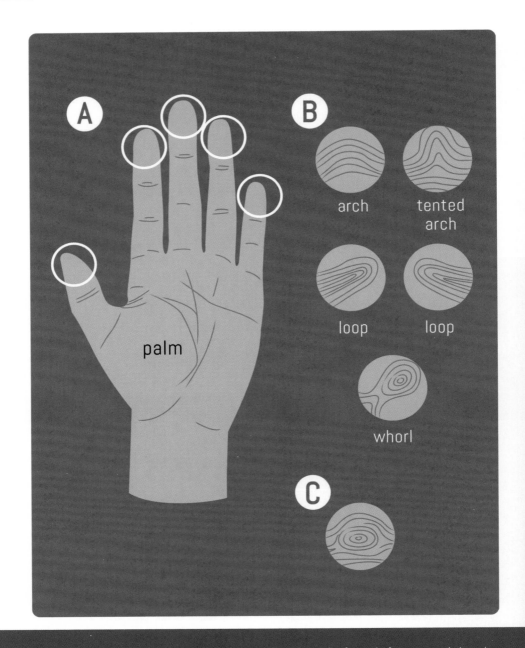

Figure 1. a) You will find a pattern of lines at the end of each finger and thumb. b) The basic fingerprint patterns are arch, loop, and whorl. c) Some prints have a combination of patterns.

and thumb (Figure 1a). Notice the pattern of curved lines. A magnifying glass will help you see them more clearly. These lines are raised ridges of skin. They are helpful when gripping objects.

2. You may see one or more of three basic patterns—arch, loop, and whorl, as shown in Figure 1b. Some fingerprints consist of a combination of patterns, such as a whorl in an arch (Figure 1c).

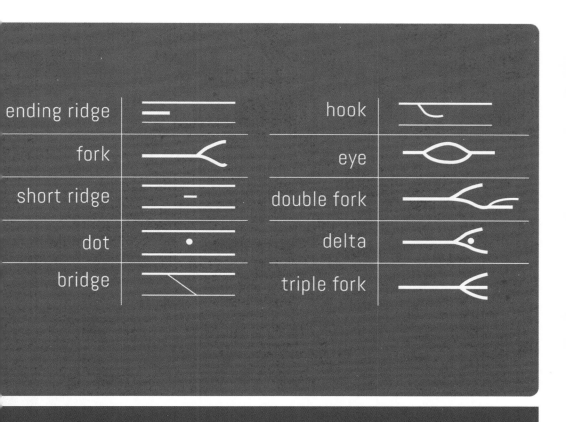

ending ridge		hook	
fork		eye	
short ridge		double fork	
dot		delta	
bridge		triple fork	

Figure 2. Details found in fingerprints make each print unique.

3. Look carefully at the fingerprint patterns on each of your fingers and thumbs. Do they all have the same pattern? How many fingers have an arch pattern? How many have a loop pattern? A whorl pattern? A combination of patterns?

4. Fingerprints may have lots of details. Figure 2 shows you some of those details. Can you find any details in your fingerprints?

5. Use your magnifying glass to look at other people's fingerprints. How do they differ from yours?

HOW POLICE RECORD FINGERPRINTS

Police use ink to record fingerprints. They roll a person's finger on an ink pad, then roll the finger on a card, which leaves the person's fingerprint as a black and white pattern that is unique to that individual. They do this for each finger and thumb. After the ink dries, they have a permanent record of a person's fingerprints. The card also has other information about the person, such as name, date of birth, place of birth, height, eye color, gender, and so on.

Many police departments now record fingerprints electronically. A scanner transfers the fingerprints to a computer database.

MAKING FINGERPRINT RECORDS

In this experiment, you will record your fingerprints as well as those of other people. To avoid the messy nature of inked fingerprints, you can use a different substance.

THINGS YOU WILL NEED

- **sharp pencil with soft lead (#2 HB is good)**
- **white paper**
- **a partner**
- **wide, clear tape (¾-inch wide or more)**
- **index card**
- **larger card, optional**
- **several people (family, classmates, friends)**

1. Using a sharp pencil with soft lead, rub the pencil on a sheet of paper. Spread a heavy layer of graphite on the paper, as shown in Figure 3a.
2. Push the end of your left index finger onto the graphite. Rub that finger all around in the graphite (Figure 3b). Push down hard. The end of your finger should become thoroughly coated with graphite.
3. Have a partner remove a length of wide, clear tape. He or she should be careful to touch only the ends of the tape.
4. The partner should place the center of the tape firmly on your coated fingertip (Figure 3c). He

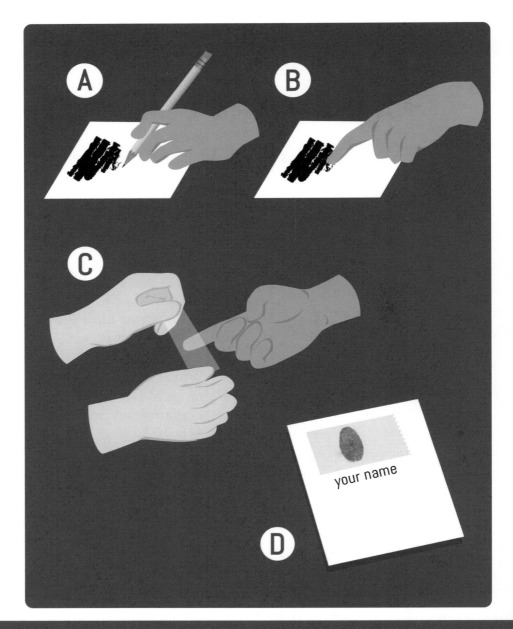

Figure 3. a) Use a pencil with very soft lead (graphite) to spread a heavy layer of graphite on a piece of white paper. b) Rub the end of your left index finger in the graphite. c) Remove the fingerprint with clear, wide, plastic tape. d) Place the tape carrying the fingerprint on an index card.

should then remove the tape and stick it on an index card (Figure 3d).

5. Examine the tape on the card, which is a fingerprint record of your left index finger. Write your name and "left index finger" under the fingerprint.

6. If you wish, you and your partner can do this for each of your fingers, where the fingerprints can be taped to a larger file card or a sheet of paper. It isn't necessary to print all of your fingers; doing each can take a lot of time. In later experiments you will use only the fingerprints of left index fingers.

7. Now, record the fingerprint of your partner's left index finger. If you wish, you can record all his fingerprints.

8. Record the fingerprint of the left index finger of a number of people. They might be members of your family, classmates, or friends. Be sure to record each person's name under the fingerprint. You will need this information later.

EXPLORING ON YOUR OWN

*   Record fingerprints by pressing a person's finger against an ink pad. Then roll the finger across a file card. Compare these records with those made using graphite and clear tape. Which method do you prefer?

*   Develop other ways to record fingerprints.

- Collect at least one hundred fingerprints. What percentage are arch type? Loop type? Whorl type? A combination of types?
- Do toes have toe prints? If so, do they have the same patterns—arches, loops, and whorls?

WHAT POLICE DO WITH FINGERPRINTS

If police find fingerprints at a crime scene, the fingerprints can be sent to the FBI, where there is a computer database with millions of fingerprint records called the Integrated Automated Fingerprint Identification System (IAFIS). The computer may find possible matches to the fingerprints found at a crime scene. If it does, experts examine the possible matches. They may find twelve to fifteen points of similarity between the two fingerprints. If they do, the fingerprints can be considered a match. The person identified will be questioned by the police. He or she may or may not be guilty of the crime.

A CRIME TO SOLVE #1

Pretend that you are called to the scene of a robbery where you discover a dirty fingerprint of an index finger on a door frame that the robber pried open to enter the home (Figure 4a).

1. You photograph the fingerprint. You find that it does not match the fingerprints of anyone who lives there. You suspect it was left by the robber.

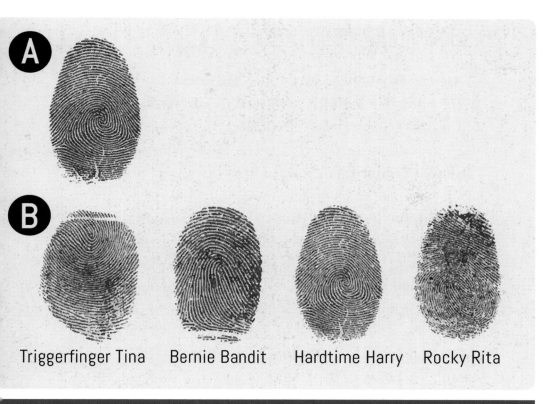

A

B

Triggerfinger Tina   Bernie Bandit   Hardtime Harry   Rocky Rita

Figure 4. a) Fingerprint you found at a crime scene. b) Fingerprints of suspects.

2. Your police department has fingerprints of previously convicted robbers on file. Four of those people are no longer in prison. Their fingerprints are made available to you with their names printed under the fingerprints (Figure 4b).

3. You examine the fingerprints. What do you conclude? Who would you bring in for questioning?

(See answer at the back of the book.)

SOME MONKEY BUSINESS

Edmond Locard, who established the first forensic science laboratory in 1910, was asked to investigate a series of thefts in a French city. He examined fingerprints taken from windows of homes that had been robbed. The fingerprints resembled human fingerprints. But Locard could see that they were not human. He believed they were those of a monkey.

In those days (early 1900s), organ-grinders were common on city streets. They turned a crank that moved a wheel across strings, creating music. Organ-grinders usually had a pet monkey. The monkey would hold a cup and accept money from people passing by. Locard had the police bring the organ-grinders and their monkeys to headquarters. All the monkeys were fingerprinted.

Locard examined the prints and quickly identified the thief. The organ grinder had taught his monkey to climb up to and enter second-story bedrooms and steal jewelry. The organ-grinder would then sell the jewelry. He was arrested and his monkey was sent to the local zoo.

LATENT FINGERPRINTS

Often there are fingerprints at a crime scene that cannot be seen. Such fingerprints are called latent fingerprints. ("Latent" is from the Latin word *latens*, meaning "to be hidden.") Forensic scientists look for surfaces where fingerprints are likely to be found such as doors, doorknobs, countertops, and furniture.

They spray these surfaces with ninhydrin, magnesium powder, cyanoacrylate (Super Glue), or other substances that stick to the fingerprints. After a few hours, any latent fingerprints become visible. If they use ninhydrin, the ninhydrin sticks to the chemicals in the fingerprints and becomes purplish. The fingerprints can then be photographed or lifted (removed).

To lift a fingerprint, clear tape is placed on the print. The chemical used to dust the print will stick to the tape. When the tape is removed, the fingerprint will be on the tape. The lifted fingerprints can then be taken to a crime lab for analysis.

EXPERIMENT 3

LIFTING FINGERPRINTS

In this experiment you will have an opportunity to lift fingerprints, a common technique used by forensic scientists.

Do this experiment under close adult supervision. You will be using powdered graphite. You should not breathe in any of the powder. Wear a dust mask.

1. Place a clean, flat, white dish on a sheet of newspaper.
2. Rub your right index finger along the side of your nose or forehead. Then press the same finger against the center of the white dish (Figure 5a). By turning

the dish in different ways in the light, you may be able to see the fingerprint.

3. **Put on safety glasses, a dust mask, and plastic gloves.**

4. Carefully add a small amount of graphite powder near, **not on**, the fingerprint.

5. Dip a small piece of soft cotton into the graphite. You might use a clean art paint brush with **soft** bristles instead. Use the cotton or brush to gently spread graphite lightly over the fingerprint (Figure 5b). Spread the graphite in all directions over the fingerprint. This will allow the graphite to stick to as many fingerprint ridges as possible.

6. Place a length of clear, wide, plastic tape on the fingerprint you dusted with graphite (Figure 5c). Be sure you do not touch the part of the tape used to cover the print. Smooth the tape against the print with a fingernail.

7. Carefully remove the tape. Put the tape, with the fingerprint you have lifted, on a sheet of white paper (Figure 5d). You should see a fingerprint that is clearly visible. If not, repeat the process. Lifting

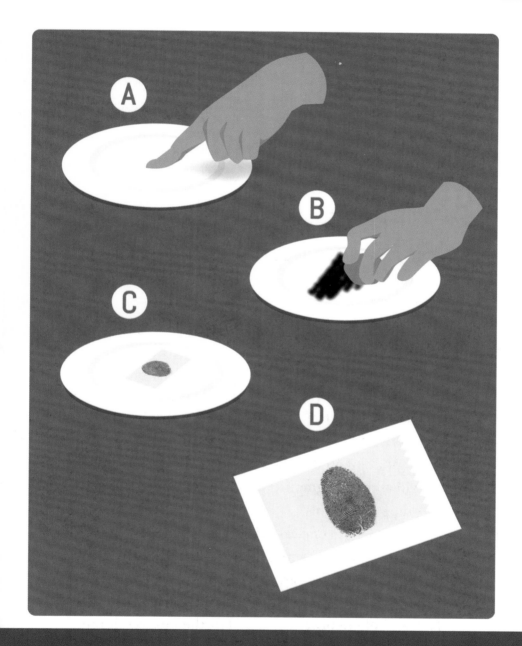

Figure 5. a) Make a fingerprint on a white dish. b) Dust the fingerprint. Use soft cotton to spread the graphite over the print. c) Lift the fingerprint with wide, clear, vise plastic tape. d) Place the tape with the fingerprint on a piece of white paper.

fingerprints is not easy. Even forensic scientists often fail to lift a complete fingerprint. You may need to practice the lifting process several times.

8. Compare the lifted fingerprint with your fingerprint record—the one you made in Experiment 1. Are the fingerprints the same?

EXPLORING ON YOUR OWN

- Collect fingerprints and toeprints from a friend or a family member. Do toeprints and fingerprints match?

EXPERIMENT 4

USING CHEMISTRY TO SEE A LATENT FINGERPRINT

Forensic scientists sometimes use chemicals to see latent fingerprints. In this experiment you will use cyanoacrylate to see a latent fingerprint. Cyanoacrylate is the chemical found in superglue.

An adult must help you with this experiment.

THINGS YOU WILL NEED

- **an adult**
- **small plastic box such as the kind toothpicks sometimes come in. (The box must be one you can seal.)**
- **aluminum foil**
- **clear tape**
- **your fingerprint from Experiment 1**
- **superglue**

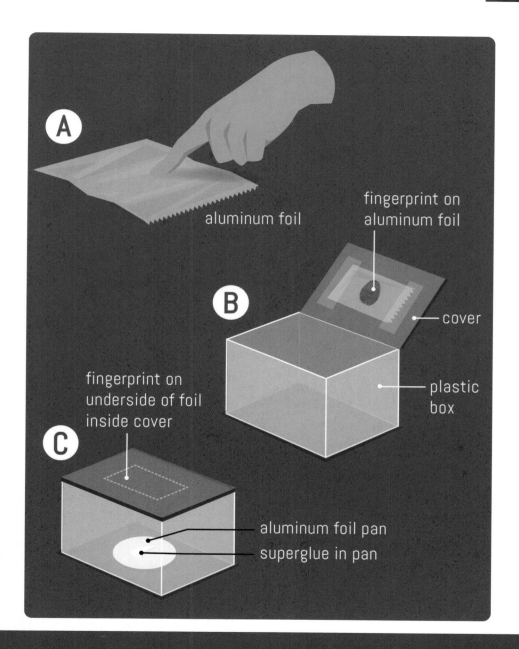

A

aluminum foil

fingerprint on
aluminum foil

B

cover

fingerprint on
underside of foil
inside cover

plastic
box

C

aluminum foil pan
superglue in pan

Figure 6. a) Make a latent fingerprint on a piece of aluminum foil. b) Tape the foil to the inside of a plastic box's cover. c) Expose the fingerprint to superglue fumes in the sealed box.

1. Find a small plastic box with a lid. The box should be one you can seal.
2. Rub your left index finger along the side of your nose or your forehead. Use that finger to make a fingerprint on a small piece of aluminum foil (Figure 6a). Be careful not to re-touch the fingerprint part of the aluminum foil.
3. Tape the foil to the inside of the box's lid (Figure 6b). The side of the foil with the fingerprint should be exposed (facing up, as seen in the drawing).
4. Fold another piece of aluminum foil to make a small pan. Put the pan on the bottom of the box.
5. **Ask an adult** to squeeze about 20 drops of super-glue into the little pan. **Warn the adult: Don't get superglue on your fingers. It joins everything it touches!**
6. Seal the box (Figure 6c) with clear tape. The cyanoacrylate fumes will slowly collect on the body oils in the fingerprint. Allow four to five hours for the grayish-white print to develop.
7. Open the box. Examine the aluminum foil taped to the box's top. You should see a fingerprint.
8. Compare the fingerprint with a record of your fingerprint—the one you made in Experiment 2. Are the fingerprint patterns the same?
9. **Ask an adult** to wrap any remaining superglue in aluminum foil and put it in a trash can.

EXPLORING ON YOUR OWN

- Make latent fingerprints on different surfaces. You might try paper, metal, cloth, wood, and others. From which surfaces can you lift fingerprints? From which surfaces is it difficult to lift fingerprints? **Do this under adult supervision. Do not breathe in powdered graphite. Wear a dust mask and plastic gloves.**
- Examine the paws of a dog or cat. Do these animals have markings that resemble fingerprints?

A CRIME TO SOLVE #2

You are called to the scene of a robbery. You discover a thumb print on the glass sliding door where the robber entered (Figure 7a). You use a piece of tape to lift the print. It does not match the thumbprints of anyone who lives there. You suspect it was left by the robber.

1. The local police department provides you with thumbprints of four burglary suspects (Figure 7b).
2. Next to each print is the name of the person from whom the thumbprint was obtained.

What do you conclude? Which suspect would you bring in for questioning?

(See answer at the back of the book.)

A

B

Louie the Louse   Ronnie the Rat   Counterfeit Cindy   Sneaky Sue

Figure 7. a) A thumbprint found at the crime scene. b) Thumbprints of four suspects.

DILLINGER AND HIS FINGERPRINTS

John Dillinger was a notorious criminal. He used acid to remove the skin from his fingertips. However, his fingerprints grew back. Police later discovered that his new fingerprints were identical to his old ones.

CHAPTER TWO

OTHER PRINTS LEFT AT CRIME SCENES

There are "prints" other than fingerprints that are sometimes left at a crime scene. In this chapter you will examine these other "markings."

As you have seen, fingers leave prints that can be visible or invisible. Other parts of your body may also leave prints. You have probably seen lip prints. Women who wear lipstick often leave lip prints on a cup or glass. After eating chocolate or ice cream, you also may have left your lip prints on a glass.

More than one crime has been solved by bite marks. Criminals who murder people sometimes bite their victims. Also, victims sometimes bite their attacker, which seems more reasonable. Forensic odontologists are sometimes able to use toothprints or bite marks to identify a criminal.

EXPERIMENT 5

LIP PRINTS

In this experiment you and others will make lip prints and then try to identify the owner of the different prints.

1. It's easy to make lip prints. Put on some bright lipstick. Rub your lips together in order to spread the color evenly across your lips.

2. Fold a sheet of white paper in half. Put the paper between your lips. Then press your lips against the paper. Don't press hard, you might smudge the print.

3. Examine the print with a magnifying glass.

   Figure 8 shows some common lip prints. Some people may have a combination of lip print patterns. What lip print pattern or combination do you see in your lips?

4. Collect lip prints from as many people as possible. You might collect lip prints from members of your

family, friends, or classmates. Label each print with the name of the person who made it.

5. Gather a group of people whose lip prints you have recorded. Ask them to have one person pretend to be a "criminal" who should leave his or her lip prints on a drinking glass after you have left the room.

6. Return to the "crime scene." Examine the lip print on the glass with a magnifying glass. Compare what you find with the lip prints you have recorded. Can you identify the "criminal" who left the lip print?

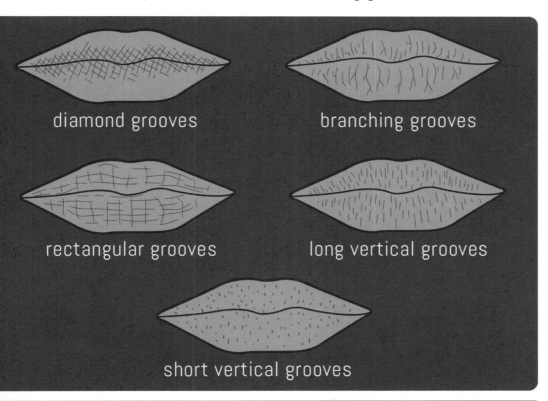

diamond grooves

branching grooves

rectangular grooves

long vertical grooves

short vertical grooves

Figure 8. Some common lip print patterns.

7. Can you use clear tape to remove a lip print left on a drinking glass?

EXPLORING ON YOUR OWN

- Collect a large number of lip prints. Do any two people have the same lip prints? Do you think lip prints could be used to identify a suspect?
- Collect lip prints from members of different families. Try to collect lip prints from as many families as possible. Does heredity seem to play a role in lip print patterns?

EXPERIMENT 6

TEETH PRINTS

Criminals sometimes leave prints of their teeth at a crime scene. It could be in the skin of a victim or in partially eaten food.

THINGS YOU WILL NEED

- **Scissors**
- **clean Styrofoam cups**
- **marking pen**
- **family members, friends, and/or classmates**
- **Gouda or other semi-soft cheese**

1. Open a package of Styrofoam cups and remove several of them.

2. Use scissors to cut squares about 8 cm (3 in) on a side from the Styrofoam cups.

3. Put two Styrofoam squares, one on top of the other, into your mouth. Bite down firmly on the Styrofoam. Remove them from your mouth.

4. Label the top piece "Upper" and the bottom piece "Lower." Compare the teeth print impressions. What differences do you see between upper and lower toothprints?

5. Collect toothprint impressions from family members, friends, and/or classmates. Label the top and bottom teeth marks and record the name of the person who made them.

6. At a gathering of people whose toothprints you have recorded, ask them to have one person pretend to be a "criminal." That person should leave his or her toothprints on a piece of cheese after you have left the room.

   Return to the "crime scene." Examine the cheese with a magnifying glass. Compare what you find with the toothprints you have recorded. Can you identify the "criminal" who bit the cheese?

TOOTH PRINTS AND REAL CRIMES

Toohprints have been used to solve crimes. In one case, detectives found a wad of chewing gum at the scene of a murder. The stale gum had hardened and teeth marks were clearly visible. A forensic dentist made casts of the impressions in the hardened gum. The marks from the teeth that had chewed the gum did not match the victim's teeth; they did match teeth impressions made by a suspect.

Forensic scientists also were able to collect some saliva from the gum. By testing the saliva, they found it was from a person with type AB blood. Type AB blood is found in only four percent of the population. The suspect had type AB blood. Facing both kinds of evidence, the suspect confessed to the murder.

A CRIME TO SOLVE #3

This crime involves a robbery in which the robber left lip prints on a water glass.

1. A house was robbed. You are asked to investigate. You observe that someone had removed chocolate candy from a box on the kitchen counter.
2. You discover a glass by the sink. There are dark (chocolate?) lip prints on the glass. Perhaps the robber ate the candy and then drank water.
3. The people who live in the house tell you they had not opened the box of candy. You conclude the robber left the lip prints.
4. You ask local police officers to help. They arrest three suspects who were seen near the house that was

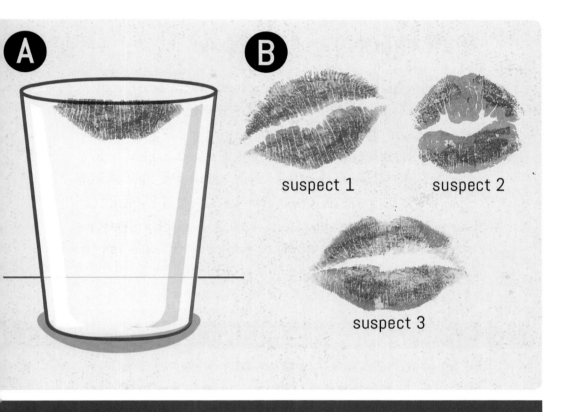

Figure 9. a) Lip prints left on a glass by a robber. b) Lip prints of three suspects. Which, if any, of the three should be brought in for questioning?

robbed. You collect lip prints from each suspect. You compare their lip prints with the ones on the glass (Figure 9). What do you conclude? What additional evidence would you seek?

(See answer at the back of the book.)

FOOTPRINTS

Criminals may avoid leaving fingerprints by wearing gloves but they often leave other "marks." Their cars may leave tire tracks on driveways, lawns, or pavement. Such tracks will match the tires on their cars. Criminals can't fly, so they may leave footprints that match shoes in their closets. Shoe tracks may be seen in snow, on muddy or soft dirt, on slushy sidewalks, or on dusty floors. Soil, dust, and stones may stick to their shoes or tires. Forensic scientists may trace such evidence back to the crime scene.

EXPERIMENT 7

FOOTPRINT EVIDENCE

In this experiment, you will try to identify the person who left a footprint.

1. Pour a thin layer of moist soil or fine, damp beach sand into a cardboard box that is at least 12 inches (30 cm) long.

THINGS YOU WILL NEED

- **moist soil**
- **cardboard box that is at least 12 inches (30 cm) long**
- **group of people—family, classmates, or friends**
- **brush**
- **waste basket**
- **ruler**

2. At a gathering of a group of people—family, classmates, or friends. Ask that one of them pretend to be a "criminal." After you leave the room, the "criminal" is to step into the box and leave a shoe print in the soil. The "criminal" will then brush off his or her shoe before you return.

3. When you return, examine the footprint. Was it made by a right or a left foot? Do you think it was made by a man? A woman? A boy? A girl?

4. Examine the bottoms of the shoes of the group. Compare the shoes with the footprint. Can you identify the "criminal"?

EXPERIMENT 8

TOOL MARKS

When a criminal uses a pry bar or other tool to break open a door or window, the tool will leave marks. The marks made by a tool in the possession of a suspect can be compared with those found at the crime scene. If the marks are similar, they may be used as evidence.

THINGS YOU WILL NEED

- **coins or candy**
- **wooden box**
- **nails**
- **tool such as a hammer, screwdriver, large nails, chisel, pliers, wrench, or file**
- **friend or family member**

1. Put some coins or candy inside a wooden box.
2. Then nail a top securely to the box.
3. Place some of the tools you have collected near the box.
4. Tell a friend or family member that the box contains something they like and that they can have it just by opening the box using the tools near the box. The opening is to be done in your absence, and the tools used are to be left along with the box.
5. When you return, examine the box carefully for tool marks. Try to determine which tool or tools were used to open the box.
6. After your investigation, tell your friend or family member how you think the box was opened. Were you right?

EXPERIMENT 9

LOOKING FOR TRACKS

Tracks are very common. In this experiment you will look for tracks and try to identify them.

THINGS YOU WILL NEED

- **safe outdoor area**
- **adult partner**

1. Go on a track hunt with an adult. You can probably find lots of tracks in light snow, soft or muddy soil, loose dirt, damp

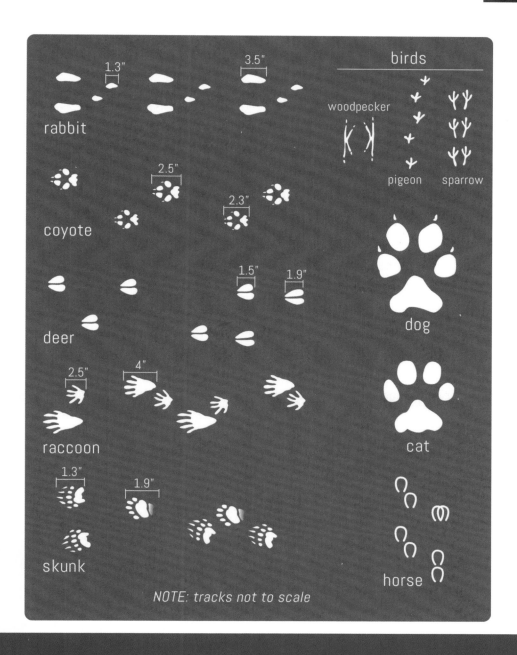

Figure 10. Tracks of some common animals are shown in these drawings.

pavement, dusty porch or patio floors, and other places.

2. Can you identify the tracks you found? Were they made by humans? Animals? Cars or trucks? Raindrops? Other things?

3. Look for tire tracks. Were they made by a car? A truck? A bicycle? Something else?

4. Look for human tracks. Were they made by a man, a woman, a child? How can you tell?

5. Estimate the shoe sizes of the people who left footprints.

6. Figure 10 shows tracks made by a number of different animals. Dog, cat, and bird tracks are the ones most often seen. How many tracks of different animals can you find around your home? What animals made them?

A CRIME TO SOLVE #4

A neighborhood family is concerned. They put their garbage and trash barrels out every Monday evening. The waste disposal truck comes by early the next morning. When they go out to bring the barrels back in, there is trash and garbage all over the sidewalk.

When they complain to the waste disposal company, the company tells them the barrels had already been turned over when they arrived at sunrise. You are asked to investigate.

Figure 11. The crime scene

1. One Tuesday morning you wake up early and find a light snow has fallen.
2. You hurry to examine the crime scene, where you observe the footprints seen in Figure 11. (Use Figure 10 to help solve the crime.)
3. You tell the family you have solved the crime. What do you tell them?
   (See answer at the back of the book.)

OTHER PRINTS

"EYE PRINTS"

The patterns made by blood vessels on your retinas at the back of your eyes are also unique. Some police departments photograph the retinas of people who are arrested as well as their fingerprints. The photos are stored in a computer. The computer can quickly compare the retinal pattern of a person recently arrested with other retinal patterns stored in its memory.

Retinal scans are used by some banks to identify patrons seeking access to their safety deposit boxes. They are also used at nuclear weapons sites, missile silos, and some military sites to ensure that only people with security clearance are admitted.

VOICE PRINTS

When you speak, you emit sound waves that travel through the air. Sound waves reaching a microphone can generate electrical impulses that can be recorded and stored as a voice

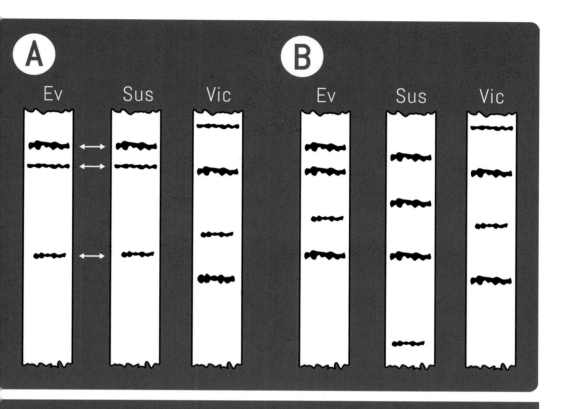

Figure 12. DNA prints from the evidence, the suspect, and the victim. a) The DNA print from the blood-cell evidence (Ev) matches the DNA print of the suspect (Sus) but not the DNA print from the victim (Vic). b) The DNA print from the evidence doesn't match the DNA print from the suspect. The suspect is probably innocent.

print. If you utter a series of words, your voice print will be different than the same words spoken by someone else.

DNA PRINTS

Forensic scientists at a crime scene may not be able to find fingerprints; however, they may find biological material such as skin, blood, sputum, semen, or bits of skin. Only tiny amounts of these materials are needed. Human cells found in these samples will contain DNA (deoxyribonucleic acid), which provides the "blueprint" that directs the development and operation of our bodies. Only identical twins have the same DNA.

DNA can be extracted from the cells and replicated many times. It is then broken into short segments by enzymes. These DNA fragments are separated into bands by electronic means. The bands are transferred to a nylon membrane and made radioactive. An X-ray film is placed over the membrane and then developed to make a visible print.

Figure 12 shows portions of a DNA print made from the evidence (Ev), the suspect (Sus), and the victim (Vic). As the figure reveals, the suspect is probably innocent.

CHAPTER THREE

BODIES, BONES, BLOOD, AND BULLETS

A dead body found at a crime scene will be examined by a medical examiner. He or she will try to figure out the time and cause of death. Wounds caused by weapons often make the cause of death obvious. However, deaths due to poisoning, smothering, smoke inhalation, and other things are harder to discern. In those cases, the victim's blood, lungs, and heart may need to be examined.

Estimating time of death is sometimes difficult. Rigor mortis (stiffening of the deceased's muscles) begins about three hours after death. Lack of rigor mortis means the death occurred within approximately the last three hours. Rigor mortis starts in the face, slowly spreads to the arms, and after twelve hours, the entire body is rigid. Rigor mortis usually begins to disappear after two to three days. So if the entire body is rigid, the time of death was twelve to seventy-two hours before the body was examined.

Gravity causes a dead person's blood to slowly settle to the lowest parts of the body. If the body is on its back, blood settles in the small of the back and on the back of the neck and thighs. The blood of a face-down body settles to the front of the body. The settled blood gives the skin a bruised (bluish) appearance.

In 1925, Petrus Hauptfleisch, a native of South Africa, killed his mother. Her body lay face down for several hours before Petrus returned to stage an accident. To make the accident believable, he placed her on her back.

The medical examiner saw that blood had collected in the front of her body and realized that the body had been turned. The attempt to make the death appear accidental was discovered. Petrus was found guilty of murder.

BODY TEMPERATURE AND TIME OF DEATH

Following death, the body's temperature begins to fall if the air temperature is lower than the body temperature, which is usually about 37°C or 98°F. The temperature of a dead body drops about 1.5 degrees every hour. Medical examiners estimate time of death using the following rule:

Number of hours since death = 98.6°F minus dead body's temperature divided by 3/2 (or 1.5°/hr).

Suppose the dead body's temperature is 95.6°F. The estimated time of death would be:

$$98.6° - 95.6° = 3.0°$$
$$3.0° \div 3/2°/hr = 2 \text{ hours.}$$

As you will find, this rule can be affected by many factors.

EXPERIMENT 10

TIME OF DEATH AND BODY TEMPERATURE

The temperature of a dead body is affected by surrounding conditions. It does not always drop 1.5 degrees per hour for the first few hours. This experiment will help you to see why.

1. Record the temperature of the air in the room where you will be experimenting.
2. Add one cup of hot tap water to a plastic container. Place a thermometer in the water.
3. When the water is about 100°F (38°C), begin recording its temperature every five minutes. Continue to do this for an hour.
4. Plot a graph of the water's temperature versus time. Could the temperature of the air around a body affect its cooling rate?

5. Next, record the temperature inside a refrigerator. Then repeat this experiment with the water and thermometer in the refrigerator.

   If a dead body was found in snow, do you think it would have cooled faster than 1.5 degrees per hour? Suppose a dead body was found in the desert, where the temperature was 100°F or more. What might be the body's temperature?

EXPLORING ON YOUR OWN

- Could the amount of surface area exposed to the air affect cooling rates? Design and do an experiment to find out.
- Fat and clothing are insulators. They reduce the flow of heat. How might fat or clothing affect a body's change in temperature? Design and do experiments to find out. Foam coffee cups, newspaper, or cloth can provide insulation.

EXPERIMENT 11

A BODY IS FOUND

You are the local medical examiner. A body was found beside an old country road. You are called to examine the body.

It is the evening of a hot summer day. The air temperature is still 95°F. The body is facedown. There appear to be bruises—bluish skin—on the small of the back and on the back of the neck and thighs. You find the temperature of the body to be 95.6°F. Except for the feet, the body is in a state of rigor mortis. You believe the time of death is about twelve hours. You write a note, "Someone touched the body before I arrived."

You question all those present. No one at the scene claims to have touched the body.

Your assistant estimates the time of death to be two hours. She shows you the following calculations:

$$98.6° - 95.6° = 3°$$
$$3° \div 1.5 = 2 \text{ hours}$$

In your report, you estimate time of death to be about twelve hours. You also request that a forensic scientist look for fingerprints and trace evidence (hairs, fibers, skin cells, etc.) on the body. Why did you not accept your assistant's estimate? Why did you request a search for fingerprints and other evidence on the body?

(See answer at the back of the book.)

BONES ARE VALUABLE EVIDENCE

There are scientists, known as physical anthropologists, who search for and study the fossil bones of our ancient ancestors. When old remains are discovered, the FBI and other police often work with these scientists. The scientists help the FBI answer questions about the remains. Are the bones human? How old are they? Do the bones indicate a crime was involved? If so, was the victim male or female? Was he or she Caucasian, Black, Asian, or Native American? Was the victim tall or short? Muscular? Using the clues found in the remains, physical anthropologists can answer these questions and more.

Pelvic bones are used to determine whether the skeletal remains are those of a man or a woman. A woman's pelvis is wider and shallower than a man's (see Figure 13).

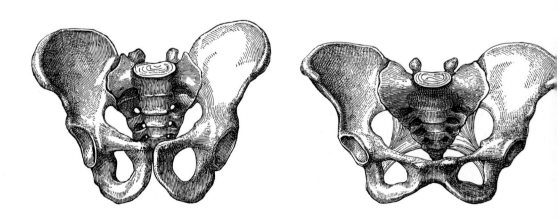

Figure 13. The bones of a man's pelvis (left) differ from the bones of a woman's pelvis (right).

If a skeleton has teeth, dental records may help to identify the remains. Height is easy to determine from a skeleton. But anthropologists have found ways to estimate height from partial skeletons using mathematics. You can do an experiment to see how this is done.

EXPERIMENT 12

FINDING HEIGHT BY MEASURING BONES

Anthropologists can estimate the height of a crime victim from skeletal remains (bones). Suppose a human femur (upper leg bone), the longest bone in the body, is found (see Figure 14). An anthropologist can estimate the victim's height using the following formula:

THINGS YOU WILL NEED

- **ruler**
- **yardstick**
- **measuring tape**
- **people**
- **calculator, optional**

Victim's height = length of femur (in inches) x 2.38 + 24.2 inches.

If the femur is 18 inches long, the estimated height of the victim would be 67 inches.

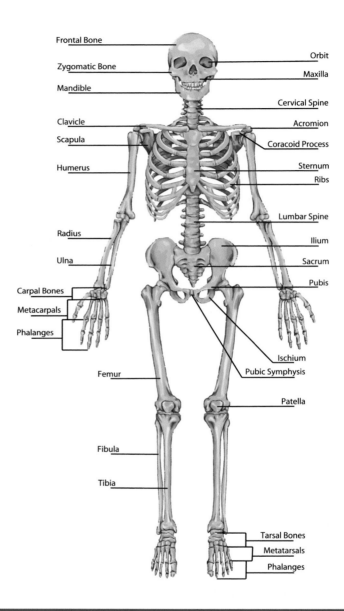

Frontal Bone

Zygomatic Bone

Mandible

Clavicle

Scapula

Humerus

Radius

Ulna

Carpal Bones

Metacarpals

Phalanges

Femur

Fibula

Tibia

Orbit

Maxilla

Cervical Spine

Acromion

Coracoid Process

Sternum

Ribs

Lumbar Spine

Ilium

Sacrum

Pubis

Ischium

Pubic Symphysis

Patella

Tarsal Bones

Metatarsals

Phalanges

Figure 14. A diagram of the human skeleton (front view).

Estimated height = (18 in x 2.38) + 24.2 in = 42.8 in + 24.2 in = 67.0 in.

You may be able to make estimates of height by measuring other bones.

1. Have someone measure your ulna. This is the bone that goes from your elbow to the small "bump" on the outside of your wrist; its upper end is your elbow (see Figure 14). How long is your ulna?

2. Divide your height in inches by the length of your ulna. Suppose your height is 54 inches and your ulna is 9 inches long. Then 54 inches divided by 9 inches = 6. The number you find may be slightly different.

3. Use the number you found to estimate people's heights by just measuring their ulnas. Suppose the number you found was 6 and someone's ulna is 8 inches long. You would estimate their height to be 6 x 8 inches = 48 inches.

4. Use this method to estimate the height of a number of people. Then measure their heights. How accurate are your estimates?

5. Try other ways of estimating height. What numbers do you get when you divide your height by your cubit bone? By your span, meaning the distance across your outstretched arms (see Figure 15)? Use those numbers to estimate people's heights.

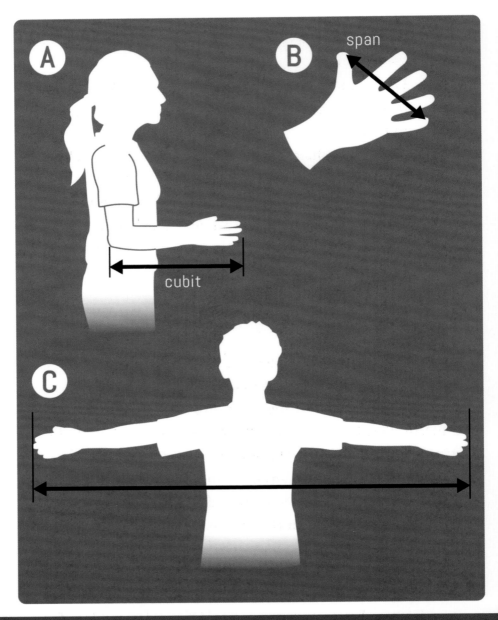

Figure 15. a) A cubit is distance from your elbow to the tip of your longest finger. b) Your span is the distance across your outstretched hand. How does it compare with the cubit? c) How does the distance across your outstretched arms compare with your height?

EXPLORING ON YOUR OWN

- Do the methods you used to estimate height work better for adults than for children? Do experiments to find out.
- Can you estimate people's height by the length of their feet?
- Can you make a good estimate of a barefoot person's height by measuring the distance from his or her knee to the floor?

TESTIMONY OF AN ANTHROPOLOGIST AT ADOLPHE LUETGERT'S TRIAL

In 1897, Dr. George Dorsey was asked to testify at the trial of Adolphe Luetgert, a Chicago sausage maker. It was probably the first time an anthropologist served as a forensic expert at a trial. Luetgert had been accused of killing his wife. He claimed the bone fragments found at the crime scene were animal bones related to his sausage making. But Dorsey identified one small bone as a sesamoid bone found in the tendon of a human big toe. Based on the size of this bone, Dorsey concluded it was from a female.

Dorsey's testimony convinced the jury that the bones were human. Luetgert was convicted of murdering his wife and sentenced to life in prison.

A CRIME TO SOLVE #5

A man's wife has disappeared. The man told friends and neighbors that she had gone to Europe to visit family and former basketball teammates. (She was a college basketball player who was six feet, two inches tall.) Two years later, she has still not returned. Neighbors are suspicious and ask police to investigate.

Police search the house and property. In the woods behind the house, they find a section of ground that appears different from its surroundings. They dig up the ground and find a skeleton.

1. As a forensic anthropologist, you are asked to examine the skeleton.
2. You carefully examine the bones shown in Figure 16.
3. You measure the femur. It is 21 inches long. What do you tell the police?

    (See answer at the back of the book.)

USING BULLETS TO SOLVE CRIMES

Ballistics is the study of bullets and guns. Forensic experts often rely on ballistics to help solve crimes. These experts look for evidence by examining the markings on bullets fired from a gun.

When rifles and pistols are made, the barrels are drilled out with a cutting tool. The tool makes a spiral groove, like the threads on a screw, only farther apart. The tool

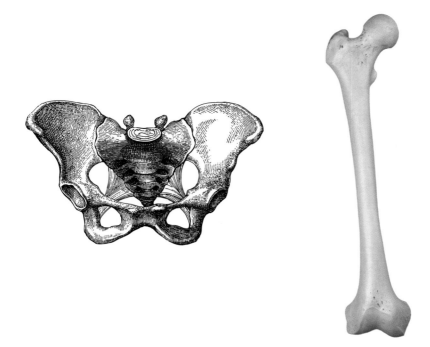

igure 16. Using these bones, can you determine the victim's height, gender, and ause of death?

leaves marks (striations) inside the barrel. When a bullet is fired, the spiral groove in the barrel makes the bullet spin. A spinning bullet travels faster and straighter than one that doesn't spin, such as a musket ball fired from a seventeenth-century gun. The barrels of these older guns were not grooved.

Bullets fired from modern guns are made slightly wider than the gun's barrel. As a result, the bullet rubs against the striations as it spirals swiftly along the barrel.

The rubbing against the striated barrel produces similar lines (striations) on the bullet. These striations are the gun's "fingerprints." No two guns produce the same markings. As the cutting tool wears with each drilling, it leaves slightly different striations.

EXPERIMENT 13

WHY MAKE A BULLET SPIN?

Do this experiment to see why a spinning bullet is superior to one that doesn't spin, such as the old musket balls used during the American Revolution.

THINGS YOU WILL NEED

- **a football**

1. Throw a football the way someone who has never seen a football might throw it, with the ball's long axis perpendicular to the ground and the throwing hand away from the laces. What kind of path does it follow? How far can you throw it?
2. Now throw it the way a quarterback would; that is, throw a spiral pass. Notice how much faster, farther, and straighter the ball travels when thrown this way. The same is true of bullets.

A MURDERER AND HIS BULLETS

Joseph Christopher was a serial killer who shot many people. He carried his gun in a paper bag so that empty shell casings would remain in the bag. In that way, shell casings that might be used as evidence would not be left at the crime scenes. However, after several murders, in his haste, he dropped several shell casings that were later found by the police.

He was captured after attempting to stab a soldier at Fort Benning, Georgia, on January 6, 1981. When police searched his home in Buffalo, New York, they found a shell casing in the basement. The firing-pin mark left on the casing matched the marks found on shell casings police had found earlier. Police also discovered part of a gun barrel that had been sawed off a rifle. The remaining part of the gun would have fit in a paper bag. Although police never found the sawed-off gun, the shell casing evidence helped to convict Christopher.

BLOOD EVIDENCE

Blood or bloodstains are often found at a crime scene or on the clothes of a suspect. Blood can be key forensic evidence. Forensic scientists look for drops or spatters of blood on a floor or wall as well as bloody fingerprints on doors, walls, and other places.

A forensic scientist will examine the pattern of spattered blood. The patterns may enable him or her to recreate part of the crime. From the shape of dried drops of blood, an expert can often tell the speed and angle at which the drops landed. He or she may also be able to decide the force of a blow or a bullet that hit the victim. Bloodstains that have been cleaned up may be made visible by spraying the area with luminol, which reacts with red blood cells and creates a bluish glow that can be seen in the dark.

Blood found at a crime scene will later be tested at a crime laboratory. If it is human blood, the blood type (A, B, AB, or O) will be determined in order to determine if it matches a victim or suspect.

BLOOD TYPES

Blood contains red blood cells and white blood cells that reside in a fluid called plasma. Not all human blood is the same. A person's blood is one of four types—A, B, AB, or O. The red blood cells of type A blood contain the A antigen; the same cells of type B blood contain the B antigen; the cells of AB blood contain both antigens, and the cells of type O blood contain neither antigen. The plasma of these blood types contain antibodies—A and/or B—that will react with the corresponding antigen, causing the cells to clump together. Type A blood plasma contains the B antibody; type B blood contains the A antibody, type AB blood contains neither antibody. (See Table 1.)

Scientists use a simple test to determine a person's blood type. Two drops of blood taken from the person are placed

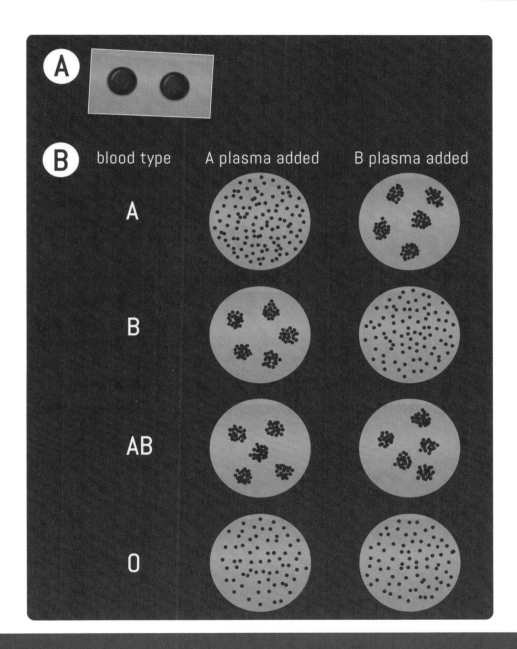

Figure 17. a) Two drops of blood were placed on a microscope slide. b) How different·blood types respond to A plasma and B plasma, as seen through a microscope.

on a microscope slide (Figure 17a). A drop of plasma from type A blood is added to one drop. A drop of plasma from type B blood is added to the other drop. Figure 17b shows what then happens to red blood cells for each of the four blood types when seen through a microscope.

Table 1: The four blood types, the antigens on their red blood cells (RBC), and the antibodies in their blood serum.

Blood type	Antigens on RBC	Antibodies in plasma
A	A	Anti-B
B	B	Anti-A
AB	A and B	Neither antibody
O	Neither antigen	Anti-A and Anti-B

As you can see, the four blood types will react differently to antibodies in the plasma of type A blood and to the antibodies in the plasma of type B blood. Type A red blood cells form clumps in the plasma of type B blood but remain apart in plasma of type A blood. Type B red blood cells clump together in plasma of type A blood, but not in the plasma of type B blood. AB red blood cells clump in both plasmas, and type O blood cells do not clump in either plasma.

Figure 17b shows what clumped and unclumped red blood cells look like when seen through a microscope. Red blood cells may contain antigen A (type A blood), antigen B (type B blood), both antigens, A and B, (type AB blood), or neither antigen (type O blood).

Table 2. Percentage of the population that is of each blood type.

Blood type	Percentage of people with that blood type
AB	3
B	9
A	42
O	46

The blood plasma of type A blood contains antibody B, which would react with the antigens in type B blood and cause clumping of the blood cells. These clumps would prevent the blood from circulating and could cause death.

Table 2 shows the percentage of people who have each blood type. As you can see, type O blood is the most common and type AB blood is the least common.

A CRIME TO SOLVE #6

1. Blood was collected at a crime scene. It was taken to a crime lab and tested. The test results indicate it is type AB blood.

2. A suspect is arrested. Two drops of his blood are placed on a microscope slide and tested. Plasma with antibody A is added to one drop. Plasma with antibody B is added to the other drop. The results, seen through a microscope, are shown in Figure 18.

   What is the suspect's blood type? Does this test prove that the suspect is guilty? Does it prove that the suspect is innocent? What would you suggest be done next?

   (See answer at the back of the book.)

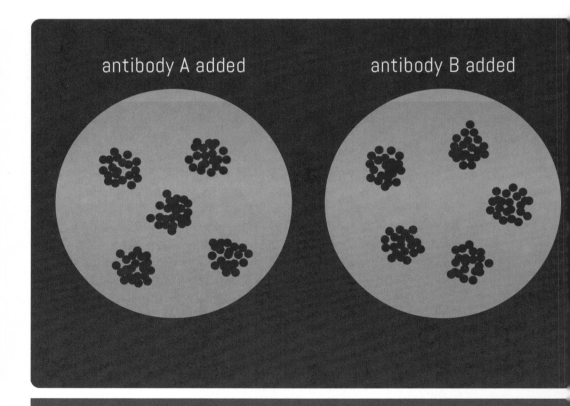

Figure 18. These are the results of a suspect's blood typing.

EXPERIMENT 14

BLOOD DROPS AND SPATTERS

Blood can provide forensic scientists with lots of evidence. Let's begin to see what can be learned from drops of blood by doing some experiments. Conduct these experiments in a garage, basement, or other place where the drops will not damage surfaces.

THINGS YOU WILL NEED

- **small glass**
- **warm water**
- **red food coloring**
- **teaspoon**
- **sugar**
- **eyedropper**
- **ruler**
- **yardstick**
- **white paper**
- **tape**
- **waxed paper**
- **board**
- **protractor**

1. Fill a small glass halfway with warm water.
2. To give the liquid the color of blood, add a few drops of red food coloring.
3. To give it the thickness (viscosity) of blood, add a heaping teaspoonful of sugar. Stir the mixture until the sugar dissolves.
4. Fill an eyedropper with the "blood" you have prepared.

5. Let a drop of "blood" from the eyedropper fall about an inch (0.5 cm) onto a sheet of white paper (see Figure 19a). What does the drop look like after it lands?

   As you can see, the drop flattens and spreads out; we say it spatters. Its new shape is called a spatter pattern.

6. Let drops of "blood" fall onto the paper from greater heights. Try heights of one foot, two feet, four feet, and six feet. How does height affect the drop's spatter pattern?

7. Make a "bloody runway" by taping six or seven sheets of paper together end to end.

8. Let moving drops fall onto the "runway." Move the eyedropper sideways over the runway as you release drops of "blood" (see Figure 19b).

   How does the horizontal (sideways) speed of the drop affect its spatter pattern? How does a combination of different heights and different horizontal speeds affect the spatter patterns of the "blood"?

   The spatter pattern of a drop moving sideways is related to Newton's First Law of Motion. The law states that moving things will continue moving along their paths unless something opposes their motion. When the bottom of the drop hits the paper, the rest of the drop continues moving forward, making small streaks or "tails" (see Figure 19c). That is why you see that some of the drop continues to move forward, making small streaks or "tails."

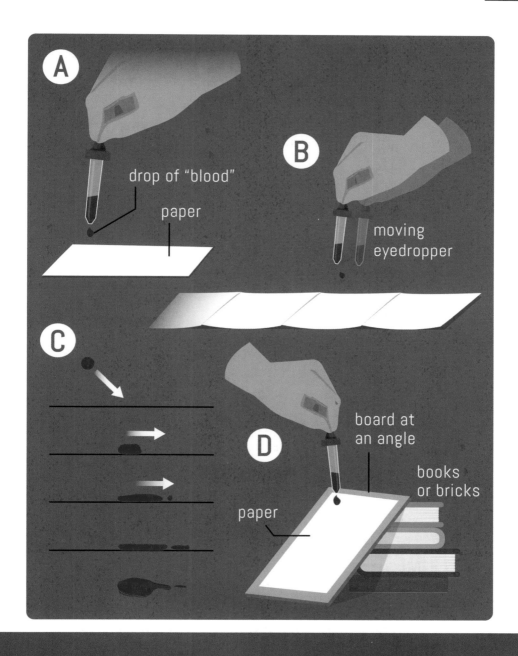

Figure 19. a) Examine the spatter patterns of drops of "blood." b–d) How does motion and angle affect the spatter pattern?

9. Let the drops fall onto waxed paper. Are the spatter patterns different on waxed paper? If so, why do you think they are different?

10. How will the angle at which a blood drop lands affect its splatter pattern? To find out, let drops fall onto paper taped to an inclined board (Figure 19d). When drops fall on the incline, they will hit the paper at an angle. How does the size of the angle affect the spatter pattern? Using a protractor, you can measure angles from 0 to 89 degrees.

EXPLORING ON YOUR OWN

- Compare spatter patterns of drops falling from different heights onto different surfaces. You might try wood, concrete, asphalt, plastic, cardboard, and waxed floors. Are the resulting spatter patterns different than the ones you have seen?

- Compare spatter patterns of drops at different horizontal speeds falling onto different surfaces. Do you see patterns different than the ones you have seen?

A CRIME TO SOLVE #7

The local police ask you, a forensic scientist, to examine the blood stain they found at a crime scene.

1. The criminal, who was wounded by the victim's scratches, ran from the scene. The police want to know in which direction he ran, to the right or to the left?
2. What do you tell them?

(See answer at the back of the book.)

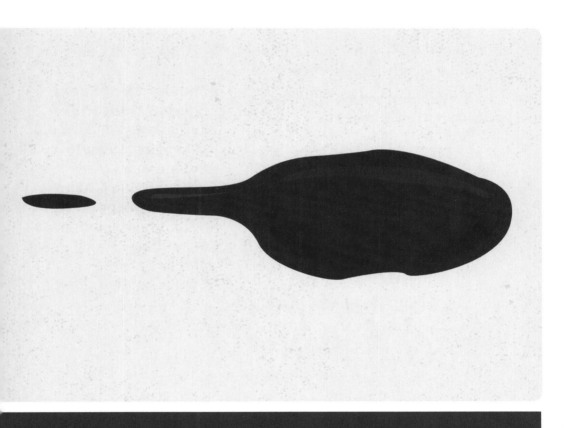

Figure 20. In which direction did the criminal run?

OTHER EVIDENCE: HAIR AND FIBERS

Careful observation at a crime scene may reveal hairs or fibers that can sometimes help solve a crime.

THINGS YOU WILL NEED

- **fibers from different types of cloth and carpets—wool, cotton, silk, nylon, acetate**
- **human hairs**
- **other people's hairs**
- **microscope or a very good magnifying glass**
- **envelopes**
- **pen or pencil**
- **dog or cat hairs**

1. Pull some fibers from different types of cloth and carpets.
2. Can you distinguish wool from cotton fibers? Cotton from silk? Nylon from acetate?
3. Use a microscope or a very good magnifying glass to examine hairs you pull from your head. Do they all look the same?
4. Compare your hair with hairs from other people such as friends and family members. Put their hairs in separate envelopes and label them with the names of the people who donated the hair.

5. Compare human hair with hairs from a dog or cat. Can you distinguish human hair from dog or cat hair?

6. Try to find hairs on furniture such as a sofa or armchair, or on clothing or carpets. Examine them closely with a microscope or hand lens. Can you distinguish animal hairs from human hairs? Can you identify the person or animal from whom the hair came?

FIBERS AND A SERIAL KILLER

After hearing a splash in a river beneath a bridge, police saw a car owned by Wayne Williams leave the bridge. Two days later, a victim, the twelfth of a serial killer, was found further down the same river. Fibers found in Williams's car matched those found on the victim's body. Fibers found on other victims matched those from Williams's bedroom carpet. After locating the company that made the carpet, they found that only 82 carpets (1 in every 7,792 carpets) of this type could be found in Georgia where these crimes took place. Another of the serial killer's victims had been found with fibers matching those in the carpet of Williams's car. The probability of another car with the same carpeting was 1 in 3,828. Consequently, the probability of victims carrying fibers from both Williams's car and bedroom was 1/7,792 x 1/3,828 or 1/29,827,776. With odds like these, the jury found Williams guilty.

CHAPTER FOUR

DOCUMENTS AND INKS

In this chapter you will learn about crimes involving written documents. You will see how handwriting can be analyzed and used as evidence. Then you will try to solve a crime that involves writing.

Forensic scientists are frequently asked to investigate crimes involving documents. Kidnappers write ransom notes, bank robbers sometimes write plans for a robbery, and forgers write and sign checks that involve other people's money. Sometimes police obtain evidence involving document crimes. Forensic scientists can use such writing as evidence in court.

EXPERIMENT **16**

INDENTED WRITING

Oftentimes, words written on a pad can be seen indented on a page beneath the original page, even after the original page is removed. You will examine such writing in this experiment.

1. Ask someone to write something on a note pad using a ballpoint pen. It might be a shopping list or a simple a reminder. The person who does the writing should tear off the page that contains his or her original writing. The note pad should be left for you to examine.

2. Hold the pad at an angle to the light from a lamp. Turn it slowly. You will see that pressure from the written words have been indented on the paper. You will probably be able to read what was written on the page that was above the one you are examining.

3. Surprise the person who did the writing. Tell the person what he or she wrote.

4. If you have difficulty reading the indented writing, try this. Gently slide the side of the soft-lead pencil back and forth across the indentations. The lead will not darken the indentations. You will see white writing against the dark-penciled background.

EXPLORING ON YOUR OWN

- Will indented writing be easier to see on damp paper? Do an experiment to find out.
- What are watermarks? Where can they be found? What makes them visible?

ELECTROSTATIC DETECTION APPARATUS (ESDA)

Even very faint indentations can be made visible with an electrostatic detection apparatus (ESDA). The electrical properties of paper are changed when it is compressed. To see the indented writing, the paper is placed on the ESDA. It is then covered tightly with a thin plastic sheet and placed between electrically charged plates. The paper becomes charged, but the charge is different where the paper is indented. The paper is then sprayed with toner (small carbon particles) and fine glass bits that stick to electric charges on the indentations. This makes the writing visible.

Police use ESDA as well as visible indented writing to solve crimes. Indented writing is valuable evidence. It can be used to solve crimes and to convince juries of a defendant's guilt.

EXPERIMENT 17

HANDWRITING

Just as no two people have the same fingerprints, no two people have the exact same handwriting. However, matching fingerprints is much easier than identifying handwriting. You will see this is true as you do this experiment.

THINGS YOU WILL NEED

- **paper**
- **pens and pencils**
- **tracing paper**
- **ruler**
- **4 or 5 classmates or members of your family**

Here are some things to look for when trying to identify someone's handwriting.

- Do the letters slant to the right or to the left? (Figure 21a) The writing of left-handed people often slants to the left.
- Do the letters slant a lot or just a little? (Figure 21b)
- Are there loops in letters such as f, g, h, j, k, l, q, and y? (Figure 21c)
- Is the writing smooth, jagged, or written by a trembling hand? (Figure 21d)
- Are some letters written with flourishes or in an unusual way? Are there unusual spaces between letters? (Figure 21e)

Figure 21. a–e) Things to look for when you examine handwriting.
f–g) Use dots to form a pattern for handwritten words.

You can also do what handwriting experts do. Make patterns from the handwriting.

1. Write your name on a sheet of paper.
2. Place a sheet of tracing paper over your name.
3. Use a pencil to make dots on the tracing paper. Put the dots at the highest point of each letter in your name.
4. Use a ruler to connect the dots. It will form a pattern like the one shown in Figure 21f.
5. Repeat the process. This time place a dot at the lowest point of each letter in your name. Again, use a ruler to connect the dots. It will form a pattern like the one shown in Figure 21g.
6. Ask friends or family members to write you brief messages. Have each person sign his or her message. Then ask them to choose one person to write an additional unsigned message.
7. Examine the handwriting on all the messages carefully. Use what you have learned to decide who wrote the unsigned message.

EXPLORING ON YOUR OWN

- Write your name so that it looks like your signature on a sheet of paper. Give the paper to someone. Ask him or her to try to forge your signature. Can you use handwriting analysis to show that it is a forgery?

- Does a person's handwriting change with age? Design an experiment to find out. (Hint: a parent or grandparent may have letters, essays, or notes they wrote many years ago that you can use for comparison purposes.)
- Can you distinguish a girl's handwriting from a boy's? Design experiments to find out.
- Can you always tell from handwriting whether or not a person is left handed? Design an experiment to find out.

A CRIME TO SOLVE #8

An army general has been kidnapped by terrorists. A ransom note was sent to the president. (Figure 22a) Four suspects have been arrested. You are called to Washington by the FBI because you are a handwriting expert.

1. You know a suspect who is guilty might try to disguise his handwriting. Consequently, you do not ask each suspect to rewrite the ransom note. Instead, you ask each to write lengthy articles that you dictate.
2. You then cut out words from each suspect's lengthy writing that match the words in the ransom note.
3. You carefully put those words together to match the ones in the ransom note. You have done this for each suspect. The results are shown in Figure 22b.

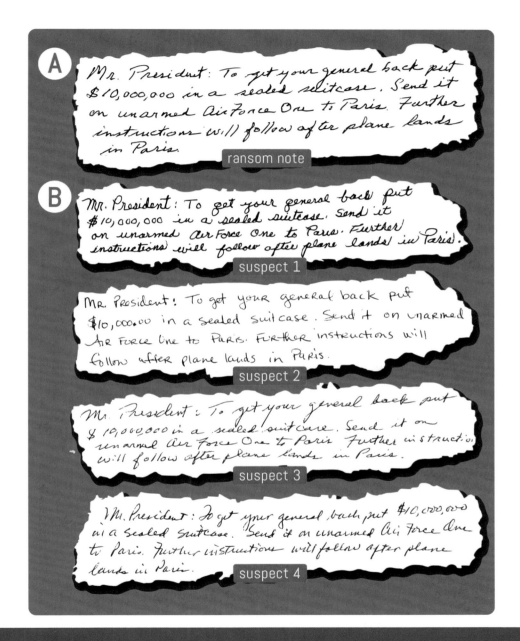

Figure 22. a) This is the ransom note sent to the president. b) Handwritten words of the four suspects are put together to re-create the ransom note.

Carefully examine the written notes in Figure 22b. Did one of the suspects write the ransom note? If you think so, which suspect was it? What evidence do you have to support your conclusion?

(See answer at the back of the book.)

INKS, CHROMATOGRAPHY, AND INVISIBLE INKS

You know that handwriting can be used as evidence. The ink used to write messages can also serve as evidence. Forensic document examiners need to know how to identify different inks and papers. You, too, can begin to learn how to identify them.

Sometimes messages can be found on seemingly blank sheets of paper. How? The writer used some form of invisible ink. Invisible inks were popular during the American Revolutionary War. General George Washington received many messages from officers under his command. Those messages were sometimes written with invisible ink. If the messenger was captured, the British would see only blank paper.

EXPERIMENT **18**

SEPARATING THE COLORS IN INK: CHROMATOGRAPHY

"Chromatography" is the combination of two Greek words: *chroma* (color) and *graphein* (to write). Chromatography allows you to separate colored chemicals in inks.

Paper is made of small wood fibers pressed tightly together, but small spaces between the fibers remain. Water and other liquids are attracted to the fibers, moving into the small spaces between fibers. For example,

THINGS YOU WILL NEED

- **black felt-tip pens of different brands**
- **fountain pens with black water-soluble ink**
- **white coffee filters or blotting paper**
- **scissors**
- **ruler**
- **water**
- **long tray or plastic dish**
- **long stick or ruler**
- **books or bricks**
- **tape**

when paper towels absorb water, the water goes into the spaces between the fibers. Chromatography works because of the small spaces between paper fibers. Liquids "climb" up through the tiny spaces between wood fibers, a phenomenon known as capillarity. Let's see how it works.

If the air where you are doing the experiment is dry, you also may need a tall jar, aluminum foil, and rubbing alcohol.

1. Collect several brands of black felt-tip pens. Also collect several different fountain pens with black ink.
2. Add about 2.5 cm (1 in) of water to a long tray or plastic dish. Fix a long stick or ruler about 15 cm (6 in) above the water. You can use books or bricks to support the stick as shown in Figure 23a.
3. Cut some strips from white coffee filters or blotting paper. The strips should be about 15 cm (6 in) long and 2.5 cm (1 in) wide. Cut one strip for each pen.
4. Use scissors to make one end of each strip arrow shaped. (Figure 23b)
5. Just above the arrow head on one strip, draw a black line with one of the pens.
6. Use tape to hang the strip with the ink line from the long stick (Figure 23c). Only a portion of the tip of the arrow should touch the water. Place the pen used to mark the strip next to the strip as shown.
7. Mark each remaining strip with a different pen. Hang each strip from the long stick. Be sure that only a portion of the tip of the arrow tip is in the water. Place the pen used to mark each strip next to the strip as shown (Figure 23d).
8. Water will move up the strips. The water will carry the colors upward. The heavier colored chemicals will move slower than the lighter ones. This will cause the colors to separate. What colors were in the ink of each brand of pen?

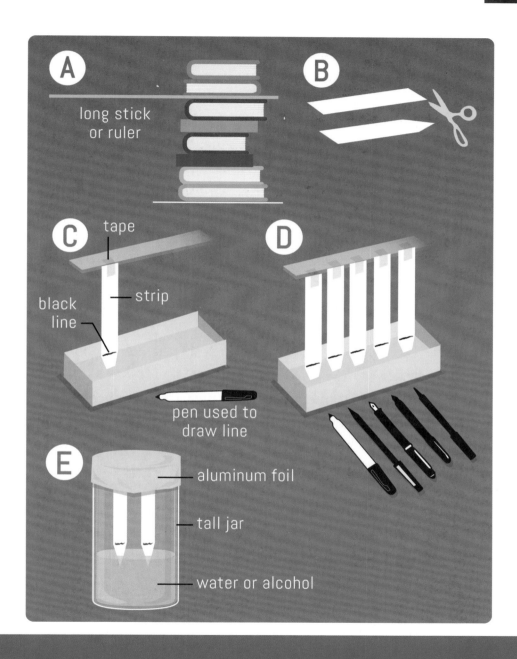

Figure 23. Make chromatograms from different black inks.

Sometimes the air is dry. The water evaporates before it carries the ink very far. Then the colors are not separated.

9. If the air is dry, hang the strips in tall jars. (Figure 23e) Cover the jar with aluminum foil. The foil will prevent water from evaporating.

10. Some inks won't dissolve in water. Colors in such inks will not move up the strip. For these inks, use rubbing alcohol in place of water.

11. After several hours, examine the strips. What colors were in each ink?

EXPLORING ON YOUR OWN

- Do food colors contain more than one colored chemical? Do experiments to find out.
- Do other colored inks (blue, green, red, etc.) contain more than one colored chemical? How about India ink?

AN INK LIBRARY

The International Ink Library is controlled by the United States Secret Service. The library has information on the chemicals found in thousands of inks. The Bureau of Alcohol, Tobacco, and Firearms (ATF) laboratory has chromatograms, similar to the ones you made, from more than three thousand different inks. These chromatograms can be compared to those produced from evidence collected by the police. Many companies that make inks also record the date that an ink was first manufactured. In several cases, this information was used to show that a fake dated document was supposedly produced before the ink on the document ever became available.

Chromatography was used in a case involving a bomb sent through the mail. The chromatogram showed that the ink on the address matched that in the pen of a suspect. The suspect was convicted and sentenced to life in prison.

EXPERIMENT 19

INVISIBLE INKS

You can be like one of George Washington's Lieutenants and send an invisible message to a friend, parent, or sibling.

1. Pour a small amount of lemon juice into a saucer. The lemon juice is your invisible ink.
2. The wide end of a flat toothpick can be your "pen." Dip the

THINGS YOU WILL NEED

- **an adult**
- **white paper**
- **lemon juice**
- **saucer**
- **flat toothpick**
- **friend, parent, brother, or sister**
- **candle**
- **candle holder**
- **kitchen sink**
- **forceps**
- **matches**

"pen" into the lemon juice. You will need to dip the pen often. Write a short invisible message on a small piece of paper.

3. Give the message to your friend, parent, brother, or sister. Tell them to put a candle in a candle holder and place it in a kitchen sink where you will reveal the contents of the message.

4. Hold the paper with tweezers. **Under adult supervision**, light the candle.

5. Move the paper back and forth keeping it well above (not in) the candle flame. The message will slowly appear. **Should the paper start to burn, drop it into the sink.**

EXPLORING ON YOUR OWN

- Can other fruit juices be used as invisible ink? Do experiments to find out.
- Can sugar dissolved in water be used as invisible ink? Do an experiment to find out.
- Can saliva be used as an invisible ink? Do an experiment to find out.

A CRIME TO SOLVE #9

A plan to help a convict escape from prison was found in a trash container. The plan was written in ink. A suspect was arrested shortly before the escape was planned. He had a Sheaffer fountain pen containing black ink in his shirt pocket.

1. You make a chromatogram from the ink in the suspect's pen (Figure 24a).
2. You compare your chromatogram with standards from a number of different pens (Figure 24b).

   Did the ink in the suspect's pen match any of the standards? If so, was the standard from a Sheaffer fountain pen?

   If the inks match, could this evidence alone prove that the suspect is guilty? If not, what other evidence would be useful?

   (See answer at the back of the book.)

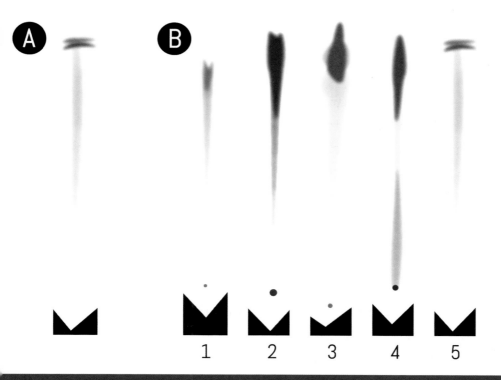

Figure 24. a) Chromatogram made from the suspect's fountain pen. b) Standard chromatograms for various fountain pens: (1) Uniball—blue ink; (2) Uniball—black ink; (3) Pilot—blue ink; (4) Pilot—black ink; (5) Sheaffer fountain pen—black ink.

CHAPTER FIVE

PAPER, FORGERY, AND COUNTERFEITING

As previously mentioned, paper is made of fibers that have been pressed together. They can be made of cotton, wood, or both kinds of fibers. Wood fibers are used in less expensive papers, such as newspaper. Fibers from cotton rags are used to make fine-grade writing paper. Less expensive writing paper has a mixture of wood and cotton fibers. Water and alcohol are attracted to the fibers and will move into the small spaces between fibers. As you have seen, this property, known as capillarity, makes chromatography possible.

Sizing is a gel made of glue, wax, or clay. It is used to coat writing paper and art paper. The sizing fills the spaces between the fibers making the paper smooth. It also prevents ink from feathering, or spreading. Ink will feather as it moves along unsized fibers.

Fine writing paper is sized. It usually has a watermark that identifies the manufacturer. United States paper money also has watermarks. Hold a five-dollar bill (printed after 2008) up to the light. You will see a faint image of a large numeral 5 in the blank space to the right of the President Lincoln's portrait and a faint image of three numeral *5s* to the left of the portrait. The images are visible from both sides of the bill.

EXPERIMENT 20

IDENTIFYING PAPER

There are many different kinds of paper. In this experiment, you'll examine several of them.

1. Collect different kinds of paper—writing, copier, wrapping, blotter, paper towels, facial tissue, facsimile (fax), note paper, and others. Try to find at least two sheets of each kind.
2. Put the different kinds in separate folders. Write the type of paper on each folder.

THINGS YOU WILL NEED

- **different kinds of paper—writing, copier, wrapping, blotter, paper towels, facial tissue, fax, note, etc.**
- **file folders**
- **pen**
- **lamp or window**
- **strong magnifying glass or a low-power microscope**
- **water**
- **saucer**
- **food coloring**
- **a partner**

3. Hold each different kind of paper up to the light from a lamp or window. Does light go through some sheets better than others?

4. Feel the papers. Are some smoother than others? If so, which is the smoothest? Which is the roughest? Record your results.

5. Make a small tear near the corner of a sheet of each kind of paper. Examine the tear with a strong magnifying glass or a low-power microscope. Can you see wood or cotton fibers? Cotton fibers may be as long as 18 mm (1.8 cm). Wood fibers are shorter, less than 4 mm. Which kinds of paper do you think are mostly wood fibers? Which are mostly cotton? Which are a mix of cotton and wood?

6. Pour some water into a saucer. Add a few drops of food coloring. Touch the torn edge of one of the papers to the colored water. Looking through a magnifying glass, watch the water go into the paper. Does the water go into some kinds of paper faster than others? If so, why do you think some paper absorbs water faster than others?

7. Use a pen to write on each kind of paper. Examine the writing with a magnifying glass. Does the ink look different on the various papers?

8. Give the second sheet of each kind of paper to a partner. Ask that person to write a note on one of the sheets. You are not to be present when the note is written.

9. After the paper with the note is returned to you, try to identify the kind of paper on which the note is written.

How might forensic scientists use paper to solve a crime?

EXPLORING ON YOUR OWN

- Investigate how paper is made. Then see if you can make paper using materials in your home.
- Test different brands of paper towels. Which brand is the best water absorber?

EXPERIMENT 21

TORN MESSAGES

Criminals often tear messages, plans, maps, photographs, and other evidence into pieces. Sometimes the pieces can be put back together like a jigsaw puzzle.

THINGS YOU WILL NEED

- **wastebasket with documents that have been torn into pieces, or someone who will tear some for you.**

1. Ask permission to look at the contents of a wastebasket.
2. Search for documents that have been torn into pieces. If there are none, ask someone to tear some for you.

He or she might tear apart a picture, a letter, a bill, an ad from a magazine, or something else. The person should not tell you what was torn into pieces.

3. Now comes the hard part. Try to put the torn pieces back together. If there are glossy pieces, separate the glossy paper from the rest. 4. Pull out the large pieces of paper first. Then separate smaller pieces.

4. Finally, try to piece the documents back together. Can you fit the pieces together to make a sensible document or picture?

AN ADDRESS LABEL IN PIECES

A package was delivered to the home of John Chapman in Marshfield, Wisconsin. The package exploded. Police were able to piece together part of the handwritten address. They saw that Marshfield had been misspelled. It was spelled "Marsflld." The ink used to write the address was an unusual mixture of chemicals.

A forensic document expert believed the address had been written by a Swedish immigrant. He said Swedes would probably write Marshfield as "Marsflld." The Swedish language does not have an *sh* sound or *ie* or *ei* combinations.

Chapman and John Magnuson, a Swedish farmer, had argued about a drainage ditch. Police searched Magnuson's barn. They found wood and metal similar to that used in the bomb.

Magnuson was asked to write some dictated words. He misspelled Marshfield as Marsflld. The ink in his pen matched that used to address the package. A forensic expert said that his handwriting matched that on the address. Magnuson was found guilty and spent the rest of his life in prison.

A CRIME TO SOLVE #10

A bank was robbed. One of the bank's tellers saw the license plate of the getaway car. The next day police found the abandoned car. On the car's floor they discovered a note that had been torn into pieces. (Figure 25) As a forensic scientist, you have been asked to put the pieces together and determine if the note is related to the crime.

1. Use a copier or scanner to make a copy of Figure 25.
2. Using scissors, carefully cut out the pieces from the copy. **DO NOT CUT THIS BOOK!**
3. Put the pieces together so that the words make sense. What message was written? To whom was the message sent?
4. Having put the pieces together, what would you suggest the police do next?
   (See answer at the back of the book.)

FORGERY, COUNTERFEITING, AND MONEY

Some criminals make illegal copies of money. This process is called counterfeiting. They then try to use the counterfeit money to buy things. The United States Treasury prints

Figure 25. These pieces of a torn note were found in an abandoned getaway car.

paper money (bills, or bank notes) with values of $1, $5, $10, $20, $50, and $100. Each bill has the picture of a historic person on the front. The treasury works very hard to make it difficult to copy their paper money. But some criminals still attempt to produce counterfeit money, hoping people will think the bills are genuine.

Other criminals try to get rich by making and selling forged documents. They might try to sell someone a fake signature of Abraham Lincoln. Or they might go to a bank and cash a check that is not theirs by forging the owner's signature.

EXPERIMENT 22

REAL OR COUNTERFEIT?

How can you tell if paper money is real or counterfeit?

1. Look carefully at paper money such as 5, 10, and 20 dollar bills.

THINGS YOU WILL NEED

- **paper money**
- **strong magnifying lens**

2. Use a strong magnifying glass. Can you find a date near the bottom of each bill?
3. Can you see that the bill is made of fibers? Do they look like wood or cotton fibers?

4. Hold the bill up to the light. Look for a watermark. Can you see a watermark from both sides of the bill?

5. Can you find tiny letters known as microprinting? You will need a strong magnifying glass to see them.

6. Using the magnifier, can you to find a few small, colored fibers within the paper?

7. Look for serial numbers on each bill. There will be both letters and numbers. The serial numbers on each bill of the same denomination will be different.

8. What steps have been taken to make it difficult to counterfeit paper money?

EXPLORING ON YOUR OWN

- Ask someone at a bank to show you how they detect counterfeit money. What do they do when they find fake money?

DISCOVERY OF A COUNTERFEITING SCHEME

Crime stoppers are people who know about a crime and report that crime to the authorities. In June, 2000, a detective in Pueblo, Colorado, received a call from a crime stopper. The call led to the arrest of Jeremiah Hall. A search of Hall's home revealed counterfeit bills of various values. A computer and color printer had been used to make the fake money. All bills of the same denomination had the same serial number. He was charged with forgery.

The public was warned to look for counterfeit money with the serial numbers Hall had used. They were also told that the paper would have a different "feel" than real money.

EXPERIMENT 23

CHECK FORGERY

Ask your parents or guardians to help you with this experiment. You will need a check from their checkbook.

THINGS YOU WILL NEED

- **parents or guardians**
- **check from a checkbook**
- **strong magnifying lens**
- **eraser**
- **bleach**
- **cotton swab**
- **photocopier**

1. Examine the check. Notice how banks make it difficult to forge checks. Is the check colored?
2. Examine the signature line with a strong magnifying lens. It probably has microprinting. Without magnification it looks like a line.
3. What happens if you try to erase print on the check?
4. **Ask an adult** to use a cotton swab to dab a small bit of bleach to some print on the check. What happens?

5. Examine the security information on the back of the check. Photocopy both the front and back of the check. Does the security information appear when you photocopy the back of the check? What happens to the signature line when you photocopy the check?

FORGING CHECKS

The most common forgery is signing another person's name (signature) on a check. Handwriting experts can usually spot this. Forgers sometimes try to erase letters or numbers. This muddles the fibers. Changes in the fibers can be seen with a microscope. Chemicals, such as bleach, may be used to erase letters or numbers or enable someone to change them. This may discolor the check. If not, the changes may be seen in ultraviolet or infrared light. Using light from the side may make changes easier to see.

Forgers may try to add value to a check. Figure 26a shows how a 9 can be changed to 90, a 1 to a 7, and "seven" to "seventy." Such changes, made with pen and ink, may have been made with ink different than the original ink. Infrared photographs may show that the inks are different even if the color appears to be the same.

A CRIME TO SOLVE #11

A bank has asked you to examine the check seen in Figure 26b. The bank thinks a forger may have been at work.

Figure 26. a) Some ways that forgers alter the amount on checks. b) Did some commit forgery on this check?

1. Do you think the check has been forged?
2. If so, what makes you think so?
3. What will you do next?
4. What should the bank do?

(See answer at the back of the book.)

CHAPTER SIX

CODES AND CRIME

Criminals, spies, and terrorists sometimes send coded messages. They would not use Morse code, which is made up of dots and dashes. It is too common and well known. If forensic scientists discover coded messages, they have to try to "break" the code.

In this chapter, you will examine some codes and invent one of your own. Then you will try to solve a crime by "breaking" a code.

EXPERIMENT 24

USING CODES TO COMMUNICATE

To begin, examine Table 3. It provides some examples of codes that could be used by criminals.

THINGS YOU WILL NEED

- **Paper**
- **pens or pencils**
- **friend or classmate**

Table 3: Some examples of codes.

Example 1: A number represents a letter: 1 is A, 2 is B, 3 is C, … 24 is Y, 25 is X, 26 is Z.

Example 2: A number represents a letter, but in reverse order of example 1: 26 is A, 25 is B, 24 is C, … 3 is X, 2 is Y, 1 is Z.

Example 3: A message such as "HIDE THE MONEY" could be written in an up-down sequence like this:

H D	T E	M N Y	or as	HD TE MNY
I E	H	O E		IE H OE.

Example 4: A simple code would be to write words backwards and in reverse order. "HIDE THE MONEY" would be written as "YENOM EHT EDIH."

Example 5: Messages could be written using mirror writing; that is, the writing could be read by holding a mirror in front of it. Leonardo da Vinci's notebooks were written in this code.

Example 6: Each letter is assigned two numbers. The first number is from a column, the second number is from a row. As shown below, A is 11, B is 21, C is 31 … X is 35, Y is 45, Z is 55. U and V are both 15.

	1	2	3	4	5
1	a	b	c	d	e
2	f	g	h	i	j
3	k	l	m	n	o
4	p	q	r	s	t
5	uv	w	x	y	z

1. Invent a code of your own.
2. Write a message using your code.
3. Give it to a friend or classmate. Can he or she decode it? Can you decode a message that your friend writes in his or her code?

CODES USED IN WORLD WAR II

During the Second World War (1939–1945), military messages were sent in code. American decoders broke the code of the Japanese Navy. They did so shortly after the Japanese attacked Pearl Harbor on December 7, 1941. As a result, the US Navy surprised and destroyed a Japanese task force near Midway Island on June 14, 1942.

The Japanese were never able to decode US Marines Corps code. The Marines used Native American Navajos to send voice messages. These Native Americans simply spoke in a modified form of their unwritten native language. They were known as Navajo Code Talkers. Their code was never broken.

THE CODE OF THE DANCING MEN

In a Sherlock Holmes story, "The Adventure of the Dancing Men," a man reports that his wife, Elsie, became very concerned when she received notes consisting of line-like figures drawn to look like dancing men. Figure 27 shows three of the messages she received and her one reply.

Holmes knew that "e" is the most commonly used letter in the English language. Since the woman's name was Elsie, Holmes knew he could expect to see her name as E_ _ _ e within a coded message. He also knew the usage frequency of letters (from most to least) was e, t, a, o, n, i, r, s, h, d, l, u, c, m, p, f, y, w, g, b, v, j, k, q, x, z; and the most commonly paired letters were *th*, *he*, *an*, *in*, *er*, *re*, *es*, and *on*. He knew, too, that a low-frequency letter that precedes a medium-frequency letter always represents *qu*. He also knew that three rarely paired letters are a, i, and o, and that an "h" follows verbs 80 percent of the time and precedes them 20 percent of the time. Using his knowledge of language and his intellect, Holmes decoded the messages and developed a partial alphabet, shown in Figure 27b. He also decided that the little flags carried by some of the figures indicated the end of a word.

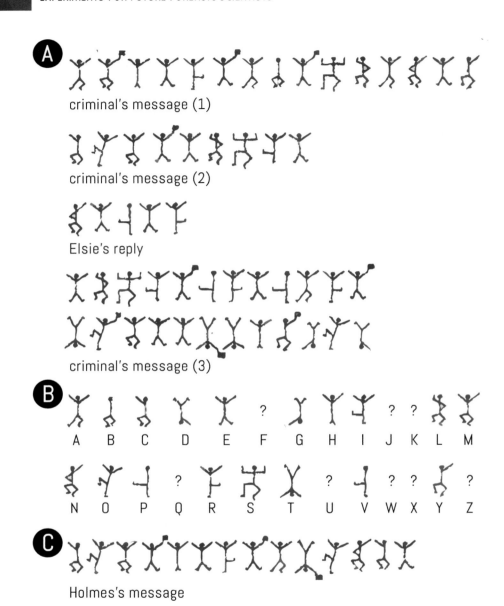

Figure 27. The dancing man was used as a code in A. Conan Doyle's story "The Adventures of the Dancing Men." Sherlock Holmes figured out the code from his knowledge of the English language. He was able to read the messages (a) once he derived a portion of the alphabet (b). What do the messages say? Holmes trapped the criminal into coming to meet him by sending him the last message (c) What was Holmes's message?

The criminal, Abe Slaney, thought the code was known only to himself and Elsie. Using this knowledge, Holmes, who decided he had to act quickly after reading Slaney's third message, was able to trap the criminal by sending him a coded message (Figure 27c). From Holmes's decoded alphabet (Figure 27b), see if you can decode the messages sent by Slaney, Elsie, and Holmes. Which message contains the criminal's name?

Why did Holmes feel he had to act quickly after reading Slaney's third message?

(See answer at the back of the book.)

EXPERIMENT 26

A NOTE IS DISCOVERED

A woman found a note on the street. (Figure 28) She took the note to a librarian who called the police.

1. The police called you, an expert on decoding, to see what you could make of the message.
2. You quickly decoded the message and told the police to be at the Oak Street Cemetery on Halloween night. There, they could recover the money from the bank robbery that took place the previous day and also capture the bank robbers.

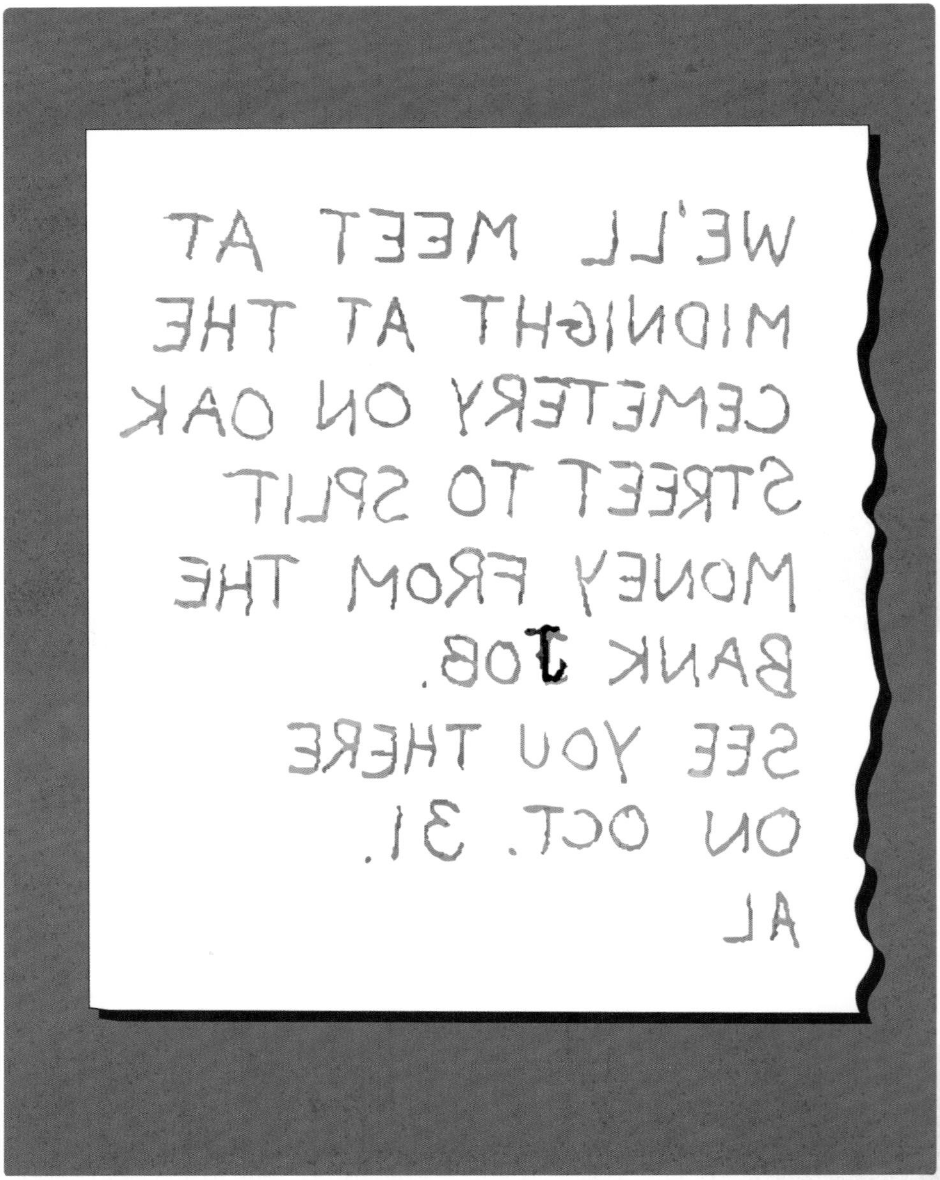

Figure 28. This note was discovered and given to a librarian.

A CRIME TO SOLVE #12

On Monday a police officer on street duty found a note (Figure 29) that was just a series of numbers. The police suspected the numbers were a code. As an expert on codes, you are called to headquarters to examine the note.

1. As a forensic expert on codes, see if you can decode the message.

25 22	26 7	7 19 22	14 26 18 13	8 7 9 22 22 7
25 26 13 16	26 7		13 18 13 22	7 12 14 12 9 9 12 4
4 22 23 13 22 8 23 26 2			11 26 9 16	7 19 22 24 26 9
12 13	12 26 16		8 7 9 22 22 7	

Figure 29. This paper with numbers on it was found by a police officer while on patrol. Is it a code? If it is, can you decode it?

2. Assuming you succeed, what will you suggest the
   police do?

   (See answer at the back of the book.)

NOT-SO-SMART CRIMINALS

Not all criminals are smart enough to invent or use codes.
Some make really dumb errors. In 1995, José Sanchez was
arrested for an armed robbery in New Jersey. During the
robbery, he used a piece of thin cardboard to wedge a bank
door open. When police removed the wedge, they discovered it was a traffic ticket that Sanchez had been given for
a traffic violation. On the ticket was his name and address.
Police had no trouble finding him.

In another case, a hitchhiker robbed the person who had
given him a ride. When he reached home, he discovered the
wallet he had stolen was empty. But his wallet, which con-
tained his name and address, was missing. He had left it in
the car with the man he had robbed.

CHAPTER SEVEN

SLEUTHING: THE SKILLS NEEDED FOR INVESTIGATING CRIMES

Forensic scientists and detectives use evidence to put together a logical and consistent picture of a crime. They must be able to separate significant evidence from that which is not important. They must be skilled observers who see all the details, ask the right questions, and recognize the unexpected when it appears. Using all the evidence, they must be able to reason creatively so as to deduce a conclusion based on all the evidence.

EXPERIMENT 27

OBSERVATION: AN IMPORTANT SKILL FOR INVESTIGATING CRIMES

In this experiment you will test your observational skills.

> ## THINGS YOU WILL NEED
>
> - **family living room**
> - **friend's home**
> - **pads and pencils**
> - **dentist's or doctor's waiting room**

1. Carefully observe your family's living room. After doing so for some time, try to answer the following questions while seated in another room.

   What pictures were hung on the walls? What books or magazines were in the room? What does the reading material suggest about the interests of your family? Is there any evidence to suggest a family pet? Is there any evidence that someone in the family smokes? If so, what do they smoke—cigarettes? A pipe? Cigars?

2. Make similar observations at a friend's home.

3. While seated in your dentist's or doctor's waiting room, try to determine his or her interests.

4. You and a friend should sit silently in a room for ten minutes. Each of you should record all the sounds

you hear, all the things you observe, and all the odors you smell. Then exchange lists. Can you now hear, see, or smell things you didn't before?

5. Observe a friend for sixty seconds while he or she observes you. Then go into separate rooms and record your observations while your friend does the same. Your list might include eye color, hair color, the side hair is parted on, scars, dimples, etc. Come back together and exchange lists. Were any of your observations incorrect? Did you make any observations that your friend had never noticed before? Did he or she make any that you had never notice before?

EXPERIMENT 28

HOW GOOD ARE YOUR OBSERVATIONAL SKILLS?

Forensic scientists observe a crime scene very carefully. They take photographs of the scene and any evidence they find. They make detailed notes, measure-

THINGS YOU WILL NEED

- **notebook**
- **pen or pencil**

ments, and drawings. They have to be sure of the location of all objects.

A careful search is made for evidence. The evidence might include a victim, a weapon, blood and other sources of DNA, hair, fibers, tooth marks, tool marks, glass, paint chips, bullets, fingerprints, and more. After going over the evidence, detectives and forensic scientists will eventually form a hypothesis about the crime. Their hypothesis must explain the evidence using sound and consistent reasoning. But they must keep an open mind. A different hypothesis might also explain the evidence and lead to a different conclusion. Forensic scientists have to be keen observers as they collect evidence.

Are you a keen observer? Let's find out.

1. Look closely at the drawing in Figure 30.
2. Make a list of all the things you observe in the drawing that might indicate that a crime has taken place.
3. What additional evidence would you look for and collect?
4. When you have finished, compare your list to the one in the Answers section at the back of this book. How keen an observer were you?

   (See answer at the back of the book.)

Figure 30. Is this a crime scene? What observations might make you think it is?

EXPERIMENT 29

EYEWITNESSES TO A "CRIME"

Witnesses to a crime often testify at a trial. But just how accurate is their testimony?

1. Ask your teacher for permission to put on a mock (fake) crime. Tell him or her that you are doing an experi-ment. You want to see how well eyewitnesses remember a crime scene. (With your par-ent's permission, you could do a similar experiment at a family gathering.)

2. Arrange to have a parent, a friend, classmate, or older brother or sister be the "criminal."

3. Set a time for the crime that is agreeable to you, your teacher, and the "criminal."

4. Plan to be away from your desk at the time of the "crime." Leave something of value on your desk. It might be a wallet, a watch, or something else. Be sure the "criminal" knows where your desk is located.

5. The "criminal" will boldly open the door and look around the room. He or she will walk to your desk and take the thing of value. After looking around the room again so that all your classmates can observe him or her, the "criminal" will leave.

6. After the "crime," hand each witness a sheet of paper. They were eyewitnesses to a "crime." The paper should have the questions shown below. (Use a copier to make copies as needed.) Ask the eyewitnesses to answer the questions based on what they saw.

7. Collect and compare their answers. Do they all agree?

8. A week later, hand out the questions again. How well do they remember what happened? How does time affect people's memory of an event? What can you conclude, if anything, about eyewitnesses?

QUESTIONS FOR EYEWITNESSES TO A CRIME:

1. Describe what you saw.
2. Was the robber male or female?
3. Approximately how tall was the robber?
4. Approximately what was the robber's weight and build?
5. What was the robber's hair color?
6. What was the robber's eye color?
7. What was the robber's skin color?
8. What was the robber wearing?
9. What did the robber remove from the room?
10. What else did you remember?

Crime #1: Hardtime Harry

Crime #2: Sneaky Sue

Crime #3: Suspect 1

Crime #4: Based on these footprints, it appears a raccoon is the culprit. There are also bird prints but they appear to belong to a sparrow, which would have been too small to disturb the trash cans. The human boot prints appear to be on top of the raccoon prints, meaning they were made after the raccoon had committed the "crime."

Experiment 11: A Body Is Found: In this case the assistant's calculations could be off because the weather was so warm. The normal formula used to calculate time of death using body temperature is likely flawed. The body's state of rigor mortis and the bruising of the skin is a better indicator of the time of death. The bluish bruises on the small of the back and the back of the neck and thighs suggest the victim had originally been on his or her back and that the body has been turned. Perhaps the person who turned the body left evidence that could be found with further examination.

Crime #5: The pelvis found at the crime scene indicates that it was from a woman. Given the measurement of the femur she would have been approximately 6 feet two inches tall. Given what we know of the man's wife, he should be brought in for questioning.

Crime #6: The suspect has type AB blood given the reactions to both antibodies. It does not prove the suspect is guilty but further questioning and evidence gathering is warranted. Further DNA testing could also be performed.

Crime #7: The criminal ran from right to left (or in the direction of the "tail" of the blood splatter.)

Crime #8: Suspect 3 likely wrote the note. Look at the way he writes his Ts and Ps. Also the slanting and looping of his writing is similar to the ransom note.

Crime #9: Yes, the inks match. The evidence alone is not enough to prove he is guilty, but if we knew how rare the pen was and collected more DNA evidence, we might have a stronger case.

Crime #10: The letter reads:

Memo:

From: I.M. Robber

20 Robbers Lane

Crime City, CT 06000

Regarding Crime City First National Bank

To: All members of the gang

The Plan

1. The guard goes for coffee at 10:30. Safe is open.
2. We hit the bank at 10:33. We wear masks. Carry guns.
3. Bob: Park car next to bank at 10:35.
4. Bill: Watch for cops at the door.
5. Al: Get dough from tall teller
6. Joe: Get all bank workers behind tall teller. Keep them covered.

7. I'll go into safe with bags fill them and come out.

8. Bill: Cover us as we leave.

9. Go to our hideout.

10. Split the money and separate.

The message was sent to "all members of the gang." From here the police could use the names of the individuals listed to see whether there are records of a gang with those names. They may also consider questioning the "tall teller" to see if he was in on the job.

Crime #11: Yes, the check has likely been forged, given the differences in ink and the apparent changing of the monetary total. The bank should be notified, and they can check any security footage and alert both John Doe and Sam Spade. Sam Spade may be guilty of this forgery, so police should be brought in.

Experiment 25: The Code of the Dancing Men: The first message contains the criminal's name. The second message tells Elsie to "come" and when she replies "never" the criminals final message reads "Elsie prepare to meet thy god," which is why Holmes was so alarmed and acted quickly.

Crime #12: This is a reverse alpha numeric code. The numbers correspond to the letters of the alphabet if the alphabet is written from Z to A, so that 1 = Z and 26 = A. The message reads "Be at the main street bank at nine tomorrow Wednesday … Park the car on oak street."Once you have the message, you can inform the police and they can set a trap for the criminals.

Experiment 28: How Good Are Your Observational Skills? Here are some possible observations from Figure 30. What did you miss? Did you see something we didn't?

The safe is open. Money lies in front of the safe. The window is open even though the snowman reveals it is winter. There's a footprint beneath the open window. Red drops on the floor and the open window could be blood. Picture is askew. Wastebasket is tipped over. A drawer is removed from the desk. The cup on the desk is tipped over and a liquid (coffee?) spilled. The phone is disconnected and the line is cut. There is a broken chair. An open safe, paper money, open window, footprint, possible blood, tilted picture, spilled wastebasket, desk drawer, spilled coffee, and the phone off the hook with the line cut all suggest a crime. Evidence to look for and test: fingerprints on various items that must have been touched, analysis of blood, photo of footprint.

GLOSSARY

chromatography A method used to separate chemicals using paper and liquid.

cyanoacrylate The chemical in Super Glue. It is used to make latent fingerprints visible.

DNA Deoxyribonucleic acid contains the blueprint for the development of a human..

feathering The spreading of ink as it moves along unsized fibers.

forgery Making something such as a document or signature that is not genuine.

forensic scientist Someone who uses science to help solve crimes or present evidence in court.

indented writing Indentations (depressions) on a paper made by writing on a page above it.

infrared light Light that cannot be seen because its wavelength is longer than the red light that can be seen.

invisible ink An ink that cannot be seen except by heating or treating the ink with a chemical.

sizing A gelatinous substance made of glue, wax, or clay used to coat paper, making it smooth.

ultraviolet light Light that cannot be seen because its wavelength is shorter than the violet light that can be seen.

watermark A design impressed in paper during its manufacture that can be seen when the paper is held up to light.

FURTHER READING

BOOKS

Bertino, Anthony J., and Patricia Bertino. *Forensic Science: Fundamentals and Investigations (2nd Edition)*. Boston, MA: Cengage Learning. 2015.

McCrery, Nigel. *Silent Witness: The Often Gruesome but Always Fascinating History of Forensic Science*. Chicago: Chicago Review Press. 2014.

McDermid, Val. *Forensics: What Bugs, Burns, Prints, DNA, and More Tell Us About Crime*. New York: Grove Press. 2016.

Mooney, Carla. *Forensics: Uncover the Science and Technology of Crime Scene Investigation*. White River Junction, VT: Nomad Press. 2013.

WEBSITES

American Academy of Forensic Sciences
www.aafs.org
Links and information including a section for students.

MIT Open Courseware
ocw.mit.edu/high-school/
MIT's open resources for high school students interested in the sciences.

Explore Forensics
exploreforensics.co.uk
Links to topics related to Forensic Science.

CAREER INFORMATION

Big Future
bigfuture.collegeboard.org/majors-careers
A career and job based website with a focus on college majors.

Crime Scene Investigator Network
crime-scene-investigator.net/
Guidelines for collecting evidence, career information, and
   links to articles.

Forensic Science Careers
forensicscolleges.com/careers
Information on some specific branches of forensic science
   and links to colleges that offer progams.

Forensic Science Technicians
collegegrad.com/careers/forensic-science-technicians
Basic information on how to become a Forensic Scientists
   career paths.

Science Pioneers
sciencepioneers.org/students/stem-websites
Links to various STEM career websites.

WITHMYDEGREE.org
withmydegree.org/can-forensic-science-degree/
   Offers ideas for what you might do with a degree in
forensic science.

INDEX